DEFENSE
STRATEGY
FOR THE
POST-SADDAM ERA

DEFENSE STRATEGY
FOR THE
POST-SADDAM ERA

Michael E. O'Hanlon

BROOKINGS INSTITUTION PRESS
Washington, D.C.

Library of Congress Cataloging-in-Publication data
O'Hanlon, Michael E.
  Defense strategy for the post-Saddam era / Michael E. O'Hanlon.
     p. cm.
  Summary: "Offers pragmatic policy recommendations for strengthening the U.S. military's ability to respond to international crises, with engagement or deterrence, and protect American citizens while maintaining fiscal responsibility, by expanding ground forces yet containing spending, modernizing weaponry, implementing privatization and reform, and encouraging burden sharing with allies"—Provided by publisher.
  Includes bibliographical references and index.
  ISBN-13: 978-0-8157-6467-0 (pbk. : alk. paper)
  ISBN-10: 0-8157-6467-7
  1. United States—Military policy. 2. United States—Armed Forces. 3. Afghan War, 2001–4. Iraq War, 2003. 5. World politics—21st century. I. Title.

UA23.O34 2005
355'.033573—dc22   2005001645
                      9 8 7 6 5 4 3 2 1

The paper used in this publication meets minimum requirements of the American National Standard for Information Sciences—Permanence of Paper for Printed Library Materials: ANSI Z39.48-1992.

Typeset in Sabon and Myriad

Composition by OSP
Arlington, Virginia

Printed by R. R. Donnelley
Harrisonburg, Virginia

*To the brave men and women
of the U.S. armed forces*

Contents

Foreword

This short but timely book by Mike O'Hanlon follows Brookings's long-standing commitment to in-depth analysis of the federal budget and, in the case of Mike and his predecessors in the Foreign Policy Studies program, to the subject of U.S. military strategy and the defense budget.

Defense Strategy for the Post-Saddam Era is Mike's fourth such study in his ten-year tenure at Brookings and continues a series of analyses that have been written by Barry Blechman, William Kaufmann, Martin Binkin, Lawrence Korb, Joshua Epstein, and others. Mike examines broad questions such as America's two-war planning framework, the military requirements imposed by maintaining alliances or other close security relationships with some seventy countries, and the implications of Bush administration preemption doctrine for the U.S. armed forces. He also distills the lessons of the recent Afghanistan and Iraq campaigns for American defense planning.

The book looks in detail at the question of the appropriate size of U.S. ground forces. After agreeing with the administration's basic two-war logic, Mike reaches a different conclusion about how large the Army and Marine Corps should be. Arguing that the extraordinary demands of the Iraq operation are imposing huge burdens on the active and reserve forces of the Army and Marine Corps in particular, he favors adding at least an additional 40,000 ground troops to the active duty ranks of the U.S. military for the foreseeable future.

Mike focuses intently on the Iraq operation and its implications for current planning, but also assesses other contemporary issues such as the Pentagon's plan to revamp its overseas base structure, the possibility that U.S. allies might be able to pick up more of the global military burden in the years ahead, and the question of the military draft. He suggests how the Pentagon might further reduce the costs of its planned acquisition programs, cutting anticipated expenditures on large weapons platforms by making the more economical improvements that can often result from modernizing sensors, computers, communications systems, robotics, and munitions. In an effort to begin discussion of long-term policy and capabilities, Mike looks beyond the immediate operations in Iraq and Afghanistan to analyze scenarios ranging from naval conflicts in the Taiwan Strait and the Persian Gulf to war on the Korean peninsula to large-scale multilateral stabilization missions in South and Southeast Asia.

Mike thanks his research assistant, Adriana Lins de Albuquerque, as well as several anonymous external reviewers, for their help with the manuscript.

STROBE TALBOTT
President

February 2005
Washington, D.C.

ONE   # Introduction

What kind of military will the United States need in the future, and how much will it cost? In an era of apocalyptic terrorist threats and other dangers there is little doubt that the country must do what it takes to protect itself. That said, at a time of $400 billion federal budget deficits, the country must also spend wisely.

This book argues that the Bush administration's planned defense budget increase of some $20 billion a year into the foreseeable future is indeed necessary. Half of that increase accounts for inflation, roughly speaking, and the rest represents real growth in the defense budget. But in contrast to current plans, a central argument of this book is that the administration should temporarily increase the size of the country's ground forces by at least 40,000 active duty troops. This is necessary in order to treat soldiers and Marines more fairly by reducing at least modestly the frequency and length of deployments and to ensure that the extraordinarily high pace of overseas operations does not drive people out of the military, thereby putting the health of the all-volunteer armed forces at risk.[1]

Given the fiscal pressures, at the same time that it carries out this temporary increase in personnel the U.S. military must look harder than ever for ways to economize and improve efficiency in other areas of defense.

1

The need is most notable in its weapons modernization programs. Fortunately, the promise of high technology, especially with regard to electronics and computers, allows the United States to continue to innovate and improve its armed forces somewhat more economically than in the past. Once the current mission in Iraq ends or declines significantly in scope, U.S. ground forces can be scaled back to their present size or perhaps even a slightly smaller number, and it may become possible to hold real defense spending steady for a number of years. But not yet. And while a drastic reduction in U.S. forces in Iraq is possible starting in 2006 or 2007, planners cannot presume that it will occur. Indeed, in January 2005, a senior Army planner publicly acknowledged that the military is making plans to sustain troop strength in Iraq at current levels through 2006.[2]

The Strategic Backdrop

U.S. armed forces will likely remain engaged in Iraq and Afghanistan for the foreseeable future. They will also need to remain involved in deterrence missions in the Western Pacific, most notably in regard to the Korean Peninsula and the Taiwan Strait. The United States will wish to remain strongly engaged in European security as well, less because of threats to the region than because most of America's main security partners are located there. The strength, capabilities, and cohesion of the members of the NATO alliance therefore have important global implications for the United States.

But the United States does not know what if any major new wars it may have to wage in the coming years. It does not know whether its relations with the People's Republic of China (PRC) will continue to improve or again worsen, raising even the possibility of war over Taiwan. It does not know whether the current nuclear crisis with North Korea will be resolved peacefully. It cannot predict whether any other countries will allow their territories to be used by terrorist organizations bent on attacking the United States. It must contend with the remarkable degree of animosity toward the United States among most Muslim countries, particularly in the Arab world—which, though it predated President George W. Bush's administration, has worsened considerably in recent years. Additional military scenarios could be of immense importance as well. Nuclear-armed

Pakistan could wind up in either civil conflict or war against nuclear-armed India. Iran could threaten Persian Gulf shipping or threaten Israel with the nuclear arsenal it seems bent on acquiring. Saudi Arabia's stability could be called into question.

Given such uncertainty, defense planning must be based on assumptions. The important thing is to postulate circumstances that are realistic, not implausibly pessimistic or imprudently optimistic. With this approach, even though the world and the future remain uncertain, the range of plausible national security challenges and military responses can be delimited somewhat.

It is easy for defense planners to dwell on problems—that's part of their job. But there also is a great deal that is good in today's global security environment. The United States heads a remarkable and historic system of alliances. Never before has a great power elicited such support from the world's other powers and provoked so little direct opposition. After the Bush administration's internationally unpopular decision to go to war against Saddam Hussein in 2003, that conclusion may be in some jeopardy, but on balance it remains correct.

Even powers outside the Western alliance system—Russia, China, India, Indonesia—generally choose to cooperate with the United States and its allies on many security issues. They are likely to continue to do so, provided that American military power remains credible and the U.S.-led alliance system continues to uphold (however imperfectly) common values on which most countries agree. This conclusion can be jeopardized—by a United States that seems too unilateralist and too inclined to use force on multiple occasions, or by allies that seem to prefer hitching a free ride to doing their fair share to ensure international security. But what is most impressive about the Western alliance system is how strong and durable it has become. And what is most reassuring about the challenge faced by American defense planners is how little they need to worry about possible wars against any other major powers, with the significant exception of conflict with China in the Taiwan Strait. Some countries fear American military strength, and even many Americans think that U.S. military spending is excessive. But as Barry Posen convincingly argues, the United States is far from omnipotent. Past historical eras, such as those in which the European colonial powers could easily conquer distant lands, are gone forever.[3] In today's world, the United States can be understood, in Posen's phrase, to possess impressive command of the commons—air, oceans, and space—but it has a great deal of trouble contending with many conflicts on land, particularly against irregular resistance fighters.[4] The Iraq experience has reinforced this reality for those who perhaps had begun to think of the Vietnam (and Lebanon and Somalia) experiences as aberrations or as ancient history. Moreover, America's high sensitivity to casualties limits its inclination to use military force, and its highly open and democratic political system suggests that it need not be feared to the extent that many apparently do.[5] Even with Iraq, while the legality of the invasion was admittedly shaky, the Bush administration acted only when it could point to Iraq's violation of more than a dozen U.N. Security Council resolutions. So U.S. power is, even in these politically contentious times, generally a force for good in the world.

The United States benefits greatly from its global military capabilities, its alliance network, and stability in the world, but maintaining such advantages costs money. The United States presently accounts for almost half of all global military spending—to be specific, 41 percent in 2003, by the estimates of the Stockholm International Peace Research Institute. (No specific estimate, however, can be precise given uncertainty over true military spending by China and several other countries.)[6] But arguments for or against the current level of American military spending cannot be based on such a figure; they must consider the specific missions asked of the American armed forces.

U.S. Military Basics

U.S. troops and most elements of the military force structure—the number of divisions, brigades, and so forth—have declined about one-third since the later cold war years. Active duty personnel now number 1.4 million, plus about 1 million reservists, of whom about 150,000 to 200,000 have been activated at any given time in recent years (see tables 1-1 and 1-2).[7] That active duty force is not particularly large—just over half the size of China's military and not much bigger than the armed forces of India, Russia, or North Korea. But the United States has a larger military presence outside its borders than does any other country—some

Table 1-1. *Major Elements of U.S. Force Structure*

Service unit	1990	2000	2003
Army			
Active divisions	18	10	10
Reserve brigades	57	42	35
Navy			
Aircraft carriers, active (reserve)	15 (1)	11 (1)	12
Air wings, active (reserve)	13 (2)	10 (1)	10 (1)
Attack submarines	91	55	54
Surface combatants	206	116	113
Air Force			
Active fighter wings	24	12 +	12 +
Reserve fighter wings	12	7 +	7 +
Bombers	366	181	183
Marine Corps			
Marine divisions, active (reserve)	3 (1)	3 (1)	3 (1)

Source: For Army, Navy and Marine Corps numbers for 1990 and 2000, see William S. Cohen, Secretary of Defense, *Annual Report to the President and the Congress* (www.defenselink.mil/execsec/adr2000/index.html [April 13, 2004]), p. 41. For 2003 active divisions and Marine Corps, see Donald H. Rumsfeld, *2003 Secretary of Defense Annual Report to the President and the Congress* (www.defenselink.mil/execsec/adr2003/ adr2003_toc.html [March 17, 2004]), p 4. For reserve brigades, Brigadier General Rolston, Briefing at the Pentagon, February 2004. For 2003 aircraft carriers, air wings, attack submarines, and surface combatants, see "United States Navy Fact File" (www.chinfo.navy.mil/navpalib/factfile/ffiletop.html [April 13, 2004]). For 1990 and 2000 active and reserve fighter wings, see Michael E. O'Hanlon, *Defense Policy Choices for the Bush Administration 2002–2005* (Brookings, 2002) p. 7. For 2003 active and reserve fighter wings, see Steven M. Kosiak, "Analysis of the FY 2005 Defense Budget Request" (Washington: Center for Strategic and Budgetary Assessments, 2004) p. 15. For 1990 bombers, see "USAF Almanac," *Air Force Magazine*, May 1996, pp. 55. For 2000 bombers, see "USAF Almanac," *Air Force Magazine*, May 2001, pp. 55–56. For 2003 bombers, see "USAF Almanac," *Air Force Magazine*, May 2003, pp. 82–83. For 2003 Marine divisions, see Rumsfeld, *2003 Secretary of Defense Annual Report to the President and the Congress*, p. 4.

400,000 troops. It is also far more capable of projecting additional force beyond its own territory than any other country. And the quality of its armed forces is rivaled by few and equaled by none.

Republicans and Democrats generally agree about the broad contours of American military planning and sizing. Secretary of Defense Donald Rumsfeld's 2001 Quadrennial Defense Review reaffirmed the active duty troop level of about 1.4 million maintained during the Clinton administration and also retained most of the Clinton agenda for weapons modernization while adding new initiatives in areas such as missile defense,

Table 1-2. *U.S. Defense Personnel*[a]

Component	1990	2000	2004
Active duty troops	2,069	1,408	1,400
Reservists	1,128	865	876
Civilian personnel	1,070	700	746

Sources: For active duty troops as of June 30, 2000, see Office of the Secretary of Defense, *Armed Forces Strength Figures for September 30, 2004* (http://web1.whs.osd.mil/mmid/military/ms0.pdf [September 14, 2000]). For reservists and civilian personnel as of September 30, 1999, see William S. Cohen, Secretary of Defense, *Annual Report to the President and the Congress*, appendix C-1 (www.defenselink.mil/execsec/adr2000/index.html [March 29, 2003]). For the 2004 active duty troops, reservists, and civilian personnel, see "Prepared Testimony of U.S. Secretary of Defense Donald H. Rumsfeld," Senate Armed Services Committee, February 3, 2004, p. 6 (www.senate.gov/~armed_services/ statemnt/2004/February/Rumsfeld.pdf [March 10, 2004]). For National Guard and Reserves on active duty, see Department of Defense, "National Guard and Reserve Mobilized as of October 27, 2004" (www.defenselink.mil/releases/2004/nr20041027-1444.html [October 27, 2004]).

a. Thousands of uniformed personnel. Selected reserves only are shown. As of October 27, 2004, the number of National Guard and Reserve personnel on active duty was 176,044, including both units and individual augmentees. These individuals are not counted in the active duty figures given above.

advanced satellites, and unmanned vehicles. After September 11, 2001, the Bush administration sought and received a great deal more budget authority than President Clinton's defense plan called for. But a Democratic president almost certainly would also have boosted defense spending after the tragic attacks, since the existing Pentagon defense plan was underfunded. Moreover, no major Democratic candidate for president in 2004 made a campaign issue out of the enormous size of the U.S. defense budget.

That the Bush administration retained most Clinton era ideas and programs is relatively unsurprising. Although whether to buy specific weapons can be debated, the military needs many new or refurbished planes, ships, and ground vehicles because much of the existing weaponry, bought largely during the Reagan administration's military buildup, is wearing out. Maintaining America's technological edge in combat may not require every weapon now in development or production, but the advantages to maintaining a resounding superiority in weaponry are evident in the rapid victories and relatively low casualties suffered by the United States in Bosnia, Kosovo, Afghanistan, and the Iraq invasion. The talk of cutting back on ground forces that was heard during Rumsfeld's early tenure has since stopped—at least for the foreseeable future—given the challenges posed by the Iraq stabilization mission.

The nation's classified intelligence budget is included within the Pentagon budget. Its reported level of about $40 billion makes it about 10 percent of the Department of Defense (DoD) total, and that fact helps explain why many Pentagon officials recently resisted calls for a strong national intelligence director, outside of DoD, with powerful budget authority over the military's many intelligence agencies and programs. But the debate over restructuring the intelligence community is moving so fast that the issue is best left for treatment elsewhere.[8]

The Two-War Framework

Since the cold war ended, U.S. armed forces have been designed to be able to fight and win two full-scale regional wars at once. The Bush administration modified the requirement in 2001 so that only one of the victories needed to be immediate and overwhelming. The new force planning framework was dubbed "1-4-2-1,"[9] meaning that the American military would be designed to defend the homeland, maintain a presence and deterrent capability in four theaters, fight up to two wars at a time, and be capable of winning one of them overwhelmingly, by overthrowing the enemy government and occupying its territory.[10]

Even as specifics are debated and modified, the United States has maintained a two-war capability of some sort for good reason. It permits the country to fight one war without letting down its guard everywhere else and thereby undercutting its deterrent capability and perhaps increasing the likelihood of a second conflict. Given the strains on the U.S. military in Iraq and to a lesser extent in Afghanistan, this purported two-war capability is somewhat shaky today. The United States would have a hard time conducting another major operation abroad now and for the foreseeable future. But in extreme circumstances, it would still have options. Most Air Force and Navy assets are available to respond to possible crises, and in a true emergency, the Army and Marines would have several active duty divisions in the United States available for deployment, while the Army National Guard could supply several more. These units would not be rested, a considerable amount of their equipment would be inoperable and in the maintenance depot, and some of their ammunition stocks could be low. But they could still probably operate at anywhere from 50 to 80 percent of full effectiveness, constituting a substantial combat capability.

If any such second major war occurred, there would be little additional pool of units—that is, a rotation base—from which to sustain forces and ultimately to substitute forces for those sent to fight it. Any large war that required such a deployment while the Iraq operation remained substantial in scale would probably therefore immediately require full activation of the National Guard—and perhaps even consideration of extreme steps, such as a limited military draft. But at present, that option need not be considered and the quality of America's overall deterrent capability need not be seriously doubted.

So the two-war logic is still sound, and U.S. forces are still capable of backing it up. Nonetheless, with the Iraq invasion now over, 1-4-2-1 no longer seems quite the right framework for American force planning. In one sense, of course, it is still applicable, in that the last "1" is precisely the kind of operation that continues in Iraq today. But there is a need for greater flexibility in thinking about what the "2" might entail in the future. A major conflict with China over Taiwan, emphasizing naval and air assets, would be much different from a war on the Korean Peninsula; a conflict with Iran that focused on the Persian Gulf's waterways would be radically different from another land war against a country like Iraq. There is a temptation, therefore, to advocate a slogan such as 1-4-1-1-1, with the latter three "1s" describing a major naval-air confrontation, another large land war, and a large stabilization mission like that now under way in Iraq. The last chapter of this book explores some of the other scenarios that could fall within these categories.

Preemption Doctrine

To what extent might the Bush administration's preemption doctrine affect the two-war logic? That doctrine, enshrined in the fall 2002 National Security Strategy of the United States, is more accurately described as a policy of preventive war than of emergency preemption. Whatever the label, it was intended by the Bush administration to emphasize that in a world containing not only terrorist organizations but extremist states that possess weapons of mass destruction, the United States could not wait for dangers to "gather" before taking action to confront them.

The preemption doctrine is a highly controversial cornerstone on which to base American security policy.[11] In this author's view, it was counter-productive for U.S. interests because it fostered the widespread (if exaggerated) image of an America unfettered by international constraints or the need to seek legitimacy for its use of force.[12] Much of the opposition to the U.S. invasion of Iraq came from the worry that it might not be the last major "war of choice" undertaken by the Bush administration.[13]

From the strategist's and military planner's point of view, however, preemption is an option that must be retained. No U.S. president could stand by while an enemy visibly prepared to attack the country. Indeed, many American leaders have given consideration to preemptive or preventive options in the past, including President Clinton with regard to North Korea in 1994, when options for destroying North Korea's nuclear infrastructure were examined.[14]

That said, appropriate targets for preventive or preemptive attack are likely to remain relatively few. All-out war involving regime change is a very difficult option to employ, and there is little prospect that any "silver bullet" technology would make it easy to conduct effective surgical strikes against an enemy in the future, primarily because countries can hide most weapons of mass destruction from existing and planned sensors.[15] Such scenarios may become slightly more practical with certain kinds of innovative and exceptional equipment, such as unmanned aerial vehicles or long-range stealthy aircraft (not to mention the outstanding personnel needed to operate it), but they are unlikely to require large numbers of such assets and therefore unlikely to be fundamental determinants of the proper size of the U.S. armed forces. However, as witnessed in recent years from Yemen to the Philippines to Afghanistan, those scenarios do place a premium on maintaining a flexible and diverse global network of military bases as well as the political relationships needed to employ those bases when necessary. So with or without the preemptive doctrine, the basic logic of a two-war capability, not more and not less, seems appropriate for the United States in the future.

Readiness

There is little doubt that the readiness of U.S. military forces should be very high. Readiness, according to the Pentagon, refers to the ability of individual military units to perform their assigned tasks in a timely and proficient way. In other words, readiness does not refer to broad decisions about sizing or modernizing the military or properly defining military strategy. It refers instead to how well DoD's individual fighting units can carry out the missions they have been assigned to implement a strategy after the larger strategic decisions have been made. Even viewed this way, readiness is still an extensive subject. Measuring it accurately requires a wide array of metrics, ranging from the training, competence, and even morale of personnel to the availability of spare parts, ammunition, and fuel and the condition of major equipment.

Readiness has generally been quite good since the Reagan administration. It may have suffered some decline due to the high demands of recent activities, and it was recently described by General Richard Myers, chairman of the Joint Chiefs of Staff, as "good" rather than the more customary "high" or "excellent."[16] But on the whole, readiness funding (and military pay, one key to keeping good people) has been consistently protected throughout the last quarter-century.

Some indicators are worrisome, such as the recent increase in the number of serious aircraft accidents.[17] But at the same time, Air Force Chief of Staff John Jumper noted that fourteen of twenty aircraft systems improved their overall readiness ("mission capable") rates in 2003 relative to rates in 2002, and he also noted that other indicators suggested that readiness had not declined since the 1990s.[18] Nor did Marine Corps aircraft show any dip in readiness.[19] And funding for readiness has been generous throughout the Bush presidency; the only threat to readiness has arisen from the high pace and strain of deployments, not lack of resources. This threat, discussed below, is serious—but it also is specific and should be solvable.

There have been occasional complaints that one administration or another abused readiness—for example, by leaving divisions unready for combat for months at a stretch—a charge that then-candidate Bush made against the Clinton administration in 2000 and that recently has been made against the Bush administration. But the need of recently deployed divisions, air wings, or carrier groups for a few weeks or months of recovery after being deployed is no surprise and generally presents little risk. The fact that several Army divisions returning from Iraq in late 2003 and early 2004 needed several months of recuperation before being certified as fully fit for combat operations, for example, probably did not pose a major risk to the United States. It could have delayed any deployment to a possible additional war in a place like Korea. But American forces still could have been sent there, in imperfect condition if necessary. In any event, South Korean military capabilities (as well as American forces normally stationed in the region) would have remained strong. So some perspective is in order.[20]

Current Deployments

Prior to September 11, 2001, the United States military had about 250,000 uniformed personnel stationed or deployed overseas at any given time. Just over half were at permanent bases; the others were on temporary assignment away from their main bases and families. In broad terms, just under 100,000 U.S. troops were in East Asia, mostly in Japan and South Korea or on ships in the Western Pacific. Just over 100,000 were in Europe—mostly in Germany but with other substantial totals in the United Kingdom and Italy. Some 25,000 were ashore or afloat in the Persian Gulf region.

Since that time, of course, deployments have increased enormously in the Central Command's (CENTCOM's) theater of responsibility, encompassing as it does Afghanistan and its environs as well as Iraq. In the last two years, there have been about 200,000 personnel in the CENTCOM zone. Altogether, these deployments made for a grand total of about 400,000 uniformed personnel overseas in one place or another (see table 1-3).[21]

The Department of Defense is planning major changes in its overseas basing.[22] Among the proposed changes are plans to reduce American forces in Korea and relocate most of those that remain south of the Han river and to move large numbers of troops that have been garrisoned in Germany either back to the United States or to smaller, less permanent bases in eastern Europe, where they would be closer to potential combat zones. More is said about these topics in chapter 3.

The Pentagon Budget

America's defense budget is, at least at first blush, staggeringly high. Specifically, 2005 U.S. national security funding is $423 billion for normal "peacetime" activities. That total includes the Department of Defense

Table 1-3. *U.S. Troops Based in Foreign Countries, Early to Mid-2004*[a]

Country or region	Number	Country or region	Number
Europe		*North Africa, Near East, and South Asia*	
Belgium	1,534	Afghanistan	14,000
Bosnia and Herzegovina	2,931	Bahrain	1,496
Germany	40,603–55,603	Kuwait	50,859
Iceland	1,754	Qatar	3,432
Italy	8,354–13,354	Iraq	130,000
Portugal	1,077	Afloat	592
Spain	1,968	Other	1,387
Turkey	1,863	Total	201,766
United Kingdom	11,801		
Afloat	2,534	Sub-Saharan Africa	770
Other	2,088	Western hemisphere	2,201
Total	76,507–96,507		
		Other foreign countries	19,421
Former Soviet Union	162		
		Total foreign countries	398,551–418,551
East Asia and Pacific			
Japan	40,045		
South Korea	40,258		
Afloat	16,601		
Other	820		
Total	97,724		

Sources: For all entries except Afghanistan, Germany, Italy, Iraq, and Kuwait, see Department of Defense, Directorate for Information and Reports (DIOR), "Active Duty Military Personnel Strengths by Regional Area and by Country (309A), March 31, 2004" (web1.whs.osd.mil/mmid/M05/hst0403.pdf [July 28, 2004]. The number for Afghanistan is an estimate based on the author's communications with the DIOR, July 2004, indicating that 12,350 troops were deployed to Afghanistan in March 2004 and on news reports that 20,000 troops were deployed there at the end of April 2004. For troop levels in April 2004, see Kathleen T. Rhem, "Operations Bringing Security to Afghanistan," *American Forces Information Service*, April 30, 2004. Since approximately 54,000 troops from the 1st Armored Division (1st AD) stationed in Germany were deployed to Iraq at the height of the invasion and 20,000 troops were deployed as of April 21, 2004, I estimate that between 20,000 and 35,000 troops from the 1st AD were deployed to Iraq at the end of March. For the number of 1st AD troops deployed at the height of the invasion, see "Statement of General James L. Jones, USMC Commander, United States European Command, before the Senate Armed Services Committee," March 4, 2004. For the number of 1st AD troops stationed in Iraq as of April 21, 2004, see General Richard B. Meyers, "Hearing of the House Armed Services Committee on Iraq's Transition to Sovereignty," April 21, 2004 (www.dtic.mil/jcs/). For Iraq, see Michael O'Hanlon and Adriana Lins de Albuquerque, "Iraq Index: Tracking Reconstruction and Security in Post-Saddam Iraq" (www.brookings.edu/iraqindex [July 28, 2004]). Number for Kuwait was arrived at by subtracting the number of troops stationed in Iraq, as well as the number of Navy and Air Force troops, from the total number of troops devoted to Operation Iraqi Freedom as presented by the DIOR, "Active Duty Military Personnel Strengths by Regional Area and by Country (309A)." The percentage of military personnel in foreign countries according to branch of the armed services is as follows: Army, 55 percent; Air Force, 17 percent; Navy, 14 percent; and Marine Corps, 14 percent.

a. Only countries with more than 1,000 troops are listed individually. The balance for each region can be found in the "Other" row. The military personnel in Kuwait and Iraq include personnel involved in Operation Iraqi Freedom. The total number of military personnel in foreign countries includes personnel involved in Operation Iraqi Freedom.

Table 1-4. *Recent Supplemental Appropriations for the Department of Defense through 2003*[a]

Date	Amount
September 2001	14
January 2002	4
August 2002	13
February 2003	10
April 2003	63
November 2003	65
Total	168

Source: Steven M. Kosiak, "Funding for Defense, Military Operations, Homeland Security, and Related Activities since 9-11," *CSBA Backgrounder* (Washington: Center for Strategic and Budgetary Assessments, January 21, 2004), p. 5.

a. Billions of dollars. Numbers do not add to total due to rounding. In addition, total costs in fiscal year 2004 exceeded supplemental funding by more than $10 billion. See General Accounting Office, *Military Operations: Fiscal Year 2004 Costs for the Global War on Terrorism Will Exceed Supplemental, Requiring DoD to Shift Funds from Other Uses*, GAO-04-915 (July 2004).

budget as well as $18 billion for the nuclear weapons activities of the Department of Energy and some smaller costs (though it does not include the budget of the Department of Homeland Security). In addition, the defense bill for 2005 includes almost $100 billion in expected funding for Iraq and Afghanistan, making for a total cost of more than $500 billion. (See table 1-4 for other recent supplemental funding bills.) The request for 2006 is $442 billion (discretionary totals for 2005 and 2006 are $421 billion and $439 billion, respectively), with again nearly $100 billion in total supplementary costs likely.[23]

As previously noted, U.S. defense spending almost equals that of the rest of the world combined, depending on how the spending of countries like China and Russia is estimated. And even after the dollar is adjusted for inflation, current U.S. spending exceeds typical levels during the cold war, when the United States faced the Soviet Union, a peer competitor with global ambitions and enormous capabilities deployed throughout much of Eurasia.

But in a broader sense, judging whether U.S. defense spending is high or low depends on the measure used. Compared with that of other countries, it is obviously enormous (see tables 1-5 and 1-6 on international comparisons). Relative to the size of the American economy, however, it remains moderate in scale by modern historical standards: about 4 percent

Table 1-5. *Global Distribution of Military Spending, 2003*[a]

Country	Defense expenditure (billions of 2005 dollars)	Global total (percent)	Running total (percent)
United States and its major security partners			
United States	410.6	40.6	40.6
Non-U.S. NATO[b]	227.8	22.5	63.1
Major Asian allies[c]	70.1	6.9	70
Other allies[d]	28.1	2.8	72.8
Other friends[e]	58.2	5.8	78.6
Others			
Russia	66.1	6.5	85.1
China	56.7	5.6	90.7
North Korea	5.6	0.6	91.3
Iran	3.1	0.3	91.6
Syria	1.5	0.1	91.7
Cuba	1.2	0.1	91.8
Libya	0.8	0.1	91.9
Remaining countries (by category)			
Asia	48.2	4.8	96.7
Europe	14.5	1.4	98.1
Middle East and North Africa	10.6	1.0	99.1
Others[f]	7.9	0.8	99.9
Total	1,011	100	100

Source: International Institute for Strategic Studies, *The Military Balance 2004/2005* (Oxford University Press, 2004), pp. 353–58.

a. Numbers may not add up due to rounding.

b. Includes the new NATO member states of Bulgaria, Estonia, Latvia, Lithuania, Romania, Slovakia, and Slovenia.

c. Includes Japan, South Korea, and Australia.

d. Includes New Zealand, Thailand, the Philippines, and the Rio Treaty countries except Cuba and the United States.

e. Includes Austria, Belize, Egypt, Guyana, Israel, Ireland, Jordan, Kuwait, Qatar, Saudi Arabia, Suriname, Sweden, Switzerland, and Taiwan.

f. Includes principally African and Caribbean countries.

of GDP, less than the level during the Reagan or even Ford and Carter administrations and only half of the typical cold war level (table 1-7). And given the relatively modest size of the U.S. military—which represents only about 8 percent of all military personnel in the world today—the budget is best understood as a means of fully and properly providing

Table 1-6. *Defense Spending by NATO and Major Formal U.S. Allies, 2003*

Country	Defense expenditure (billions of 2005 dollars)	Defense expenditure as percentage of GDP	Size of active duty armed forces (thousands)
NATO			
United States	410.6	3.7	1,427
France	46.3	2.6	101.4
United Kingdom	43.4	2.4	212.6
Germany	35.6	1.5	284.5
Italy	28.1	1.9	200
Turkey	11.8	4.9	514.8
Canada	10.3	1.2	52.3
Spain	10.1	1.2	150.7
Netherlands	8.4	1.6	53.1
Greece	7.3	4.1	177.6
Norway	4.4	2.0	26.6
Poland	4.2	2.0	163
Belgium	4.0	1.3	40.8
Denmark	3.4	1.6	22.8
Portugal	3.2	2.1	44.9
Czech Republic	1.9	2.2	57
Hungary	1.6	1.9	33.4
Romania	1.3	2.3	97.2
Slovakia	0.6	1.9	22
Bulgaria	0.5	2.4	51
Slovenia	0.4	1.4	6.5
Lithuania	0.3	1.8	1.27
Luxembourg	0.2	0.9	0.9
Latvia	0.2	1.9	4.9
Estonia	0.2	2.0	5.50
Iceland	...	...	...
Total, non-U.S. NATO	227.8	1.0[a]	2,324.8
Total, NATO	638.4	2.8[a]	3,751.8
Other major formal U.S. allies			
Japan	43.4	1.0	239.9
South Korea	14.8	2.8	686
Australia	11.9	2.3	53.6
Total	70.1	4.7[a]	980
Grand total	708.5	...	...

Source: International Institute for Strategic Studies, *The Military Balance 2004/2005* (Oxford University Press, 2004), pp. 353–55.

a. Total defense expenditure as percentage of GDP is a simple average of all countries' repsective percentages in 2003 dollars, not a weighted average.

Table 1-7. *U.S. National Security Spending in Modern Historical Perspective*[a]

Year or period	Mean spending level	Mean spending (percent of GDP)
1960s (1962–69)	382	10.7
Peak year 1968	463	9.5
1970s	315	5.9
Peak year 1970	414	8.1
1980s	379	5.8
Peak year 1989	440	5.6
1990s	359	4.1
Peak year 1991	430	5.4
2000	325	3.0
2001	328	3.0
2002	364	3.4
2003	412	3.7
2004	454	3.9
2005	445	3.8
2006	412	3.4
2007	395	3.3
2008	402	3.2
2009	412	3.2
2010	418	3.2

Sources: President George W. Bush, *Budget of the United States Government, Fiscal Year 2005: Historical Tables* (Office of Management and Budget, 2004), pp. 126–28. *Budget of the United States Government: Fiscal Year 2006*, tables 8.2 and 8.4 (www.gpoaccess.gov/usbudget/fy06/pdf/hist.pdf [February 7, 2005]. Inflation is calculated according to Budget of the United States Government: Fiscal Year 2006, table 12-1 (www.gpoaccess.gov/usbudget/fy06/sheets/12_1.xls [February 7, 2005]).

a. Discretionary outlays in billions of 2005 dollars. Peak year refers to the year when the inflation-adjusted dollar total was highest for the period in question. This table shows budget function 050, including the Department of Defense and Department of Energy, but it does not include homeland security activities except those carried out by DoD. It also includes spending for supplemental appropriations when known.

resources to the limited number of men and women in the country's armed forces. It does not reflect an American ambition to field an enormous fighting machine.

The reasons for a very large U.S. defense budget are not hard to understand. The United States has security alliances or close partnerships with more than seventy countries, featuring all of the other twenty-five members of NATO, all of the Rio Pact countries in Latin America, several allies in the Western Pacific, and roughly a dozen countries in the Persian Gulf–Mideast region. It alone among the world's powers takes seriously the need to project significant military force quickly over great distances

Figure 1-1. *Department of Defense Procurement Funding*[a]

Billions of constant 2005 dollars

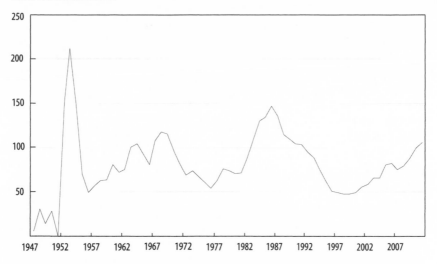

Source: Department of Defense, "National Defense Budget Estimates for FY 2005," March 2004, pp. 110–15 (www.dod.mil/comptroller/defbudget/fy2005/fy2005_greenbook.pdf [April 12, 2004]). "President Bush's FY 2006 Defense Budget," Department of Defense, February 7, 2005 (www.defenselink.mil/news/Feb2005/d20050207budget.pdf [February 7, 2005]). Inflation is calculated according to Budget of the United States Government: Fiscal Year 2006, table 12-1 (www.gpoaccess.gov/usbudget/fy06/sheets/12_1.xls [February 7, 2005]).

a. Billions of 2005 dollars. The 1951–90 cold war annual average budget authority for procurement was $94.7 billion.

for sustained periods. Indeed, as discussed further below, the United States possesses by my estimates more than two-thirds of the world's collective power projection capability and an even higher share if one focuses on high-quality military units.[24] The United States alone undergirds a collective security system that helps many countries in the Western world feel secure enough that they do not have to engage in arms races with their neighbors, launch preemptive wars of their own, or develop nuclear weapons.

Recent Growth in the U.S. Defense Budget

Still, one might ask why the annual cost of an active duty military that has grown by less than 5 percent since the Clinton administration has increased by more than $100 billion during the Bush presidency.[25] Inflation accounts for some of the growth, but the real-dollar increase in the

Table 1-8. *Department of Defense Discretionary Budget Authority, by Title*[a]

Category	2005	2006	2007	2008	2009	2010	2011
Military personnel	104.0	106.8	107.6	108.6	110.0	111.3	111.8
Operations and maintenance	137.0	144.9	148.1	151.3	154.2	155.4	156.1
Procurement	78.1	76.5	88	95.4	97.0	100.5	104.4
Research, development, testing and evaluation	68.8	68.0	64.2	62.6	66.7	62.1	52.5
Military construction	6.0	7.6	11.8	12.8	10.2	9.5	9.6
Family housing	4.1	4.1	3.7	2.8	2.5	2.4	2.4
Revolving and management funds/ other	2.1	3.1	2.3	1.6	3.5	3.1	5.2
Total	400.1	411.1	425.7	435.2	444.1	444.2	442.0

Source: "President Bush's FY 2006 Defense Budget," Department of Defense, February 7, 2005 (www.defenselink.mil/news/Feb2005/d20050207budget.pdf [February 7, 2005]). Inflation is calculated according to Budget of the United States Government: Fiscal Year 2006, table 12-1 (www.gpoaccess.gov/usbudget/fy06/sheets/12_1.xls [February 7, 2005]).

a. Billions of constant 2005 dollars. Totals are for each fiscal year and exclude supplemental appropriations. Inflation in 2011 is assumed to be the same as in 2010. Totals may not add up exactly due to rounding.

annual budget is still about $100 billion. (Note that these figures do not even count the costs of military operations in Afghanistan and Iraq.) Of the total increase, 27 percent is in military personnel costs; 27 percent for operations and maintenance; 17 percent for procurement (see figure 1-1); 25 percent for research, development, testing, and evaluation (RDT&E); and about 4 percent for nuclear weapons activities (table 1-8).

Of these totals, the increases in personnel costs are due primarily to more generous compensation packages (funds for activating reservists and for temporarily increasing the size of the active duty military come primarily from supplemental appropriations bills). Some of these allocations are more helpful for strengthening today's military than others. But as a general proposition, in a time of national crisis and high demand on the military, overall compensation must remain robust to attract and retain good people and to be fair to those who risk their lives for their country.

The operations and maintenance increases reflect the relentless upward pressure on the cost of health care, equipment maintenance, environmental cleanup, and the like. They also result from the Bush administration's decision to fund "readiness" accounts for training and equipment maintenance even more generously than the Clinton administration had done. The increases in acquisition funding are partially due to missile defense ($5 billion a year higher than under Clinton) and partially due to Secretary Rumsfeld's "transformation" initiatives (at least $5 billion annually). They also reflect efforts to restore funding for hardware to typical historical levels after a "procurement holiday" in the 1990s.

As noted, most emergency costs, including those for protecting American airspace through Operation Noble Eagle, are funded out of supplemental appropriations bills. However, some costs now found in the normal defense budget are related to 9/11 and its aftermath. The Pentagon's funding for homeland security, for example, is about $8 billion, to cover activities such as those of some 25,000 soldiers in the United States that involve protecting the homeland.[26] Similar activities overseas, such as base security, make the total for activities funded through the regular DoD budget about $10 billion annually.[27] Roughly another $5 billion may have been devoted to increases in the classified $40 billion annual intelligence budget (hidden within the Department of Defense's budget), some of which are clearly tied to the war on terror.[28] Similarly, the annual budget for special operations command has been increased by about $3 billion, to $6.6 billion (personnel totals have risen by about 5,000).[29] But even after adding up all these amounts, less than 20 percent of the $100 billion real-dollar growth in the annual Pentagon budget is due to the direct effects of the war on terror.

Further Planned Budget Increases

The era of increases in defense spending does not yet appear to be over. Expectations are for continued annual increases of about $20 billion a year—twice what is needed to compensate for the effects of inflation (or to put it differently, real budgets are expected to keep rising by about $10 billion a year, as shown in table 1-8). By 2009, the annual national security budget will exceed $500 billion—not counting the additional costs of any activities funded by supplementals and again, not counting most homeland security activities.

That means almost $450 billion when expressed in 2005 dollars. Given the administration's plans, that is a conservative estimate of what its future defense program would cost the country, even without including any added costs from future military operations or the ongoing missions in Iraq and Afghanistan. The Congressional Budget Office estimates that to fully fund the Pentagon's current plans, average annual costs from 2010 through 2020 will exceed $480 billion (in 2005 dollars) and perhaps reach as much as $530 billion.[30]

The Fiscal Backdrop

Although it must protect itself, the United States cannot afford to waste money doing so. Federal deficits, which, as noted, already exceed $400 billion a year, could exceed $500 billion annually in the next decade, even if President Bush succeeds in his goal of halving the deficit in 2009 (likely to be a temporary accomplishment at best). They would thus remain at the economically unhealthy level of around 4 percent of GDP, driving down national savings rates and increasing America's dependence on foreign investors to propel its economy. Longer-term fiscal trends are even worse, given the pending retirement of the baby boomers together with rising health care costs.[31] The United States cannot afford to buy combat formations and weapons that are not truly required.[32] If more ground forces are needed in the coming years, it becomes even more important to look for economies and trade-offs in other parts of the Pentagon budget to help fund the new requirements and avoid continued rapid growth in annual expenditures.

Indeed, in political terms, it may actually be easier to find some of those economies now—while the country is increasing its defense budget and increasing support for troops in the field—than to wait until a later period of general budgetary austerity. No one could reasonably accuse any politicians of being antidefense if they are now supporting $20 billion annual budget increases for the Department of Defense, so they may be in a better position to push for tough choices and economies today than in the future.

Containing Defense Spending While Expanding the Ground Forces

Many current trends continue to push real defense spending upward, even while troop strength is not growing. Historically, weapons costs per troop have increased at 2 percent to 3 percent a year in real, inflation-adjusted terms. A similar trend pertains in the operations and maintenance accounts. The rising cost of health care, environmental cleanup, and other such activities affects the military as much as any other sector of the economy. For example, DoD's health program budget almost doubled in real terms between 1988 and 2003, to just under $30 billion.[33] In addition, while compensation is now rather good for most troops (relative to that for civilian jobs requiring comparable experience and education), it is important that it stay that way. To attract top-notch people, military pay increases must keep up with those in civilian pay, which can require real growth of at least 1 percent a year.[34] Further increases in pay may be appropriate for specific groups, such as highly skilled technicians with much more remunerative job opportunities in the private sector, or reservists called up for active duty for extended periods who sacrifice large amounts of income as a result.[35] Fairness concerns also argue for other changes, such as a major increase in the benefit paid to the families of those who die on overseas missions (just $12,420 as of this writing).

There are several opportunities to save money within the defense budget and possibly counter these broad trends. In all probability, they will not save a great deal of money quickly. In fact, they are best viewed not as means of saving money in the literal sense at all, but of reducing the rate of defense budget growth relative to what might otherwise occur. But by this measure, they should be able to free up enough—$5 billion a year soon, perhaps two to three times as much by the decade's end—to help fund the temporary increase in troop strength that seems necessary given the demands of the Iraq mission and the war on terror.

Emphasizing Advanced Electronics and Computers in Defense Modernization

Weapons purchases are one reason that the Pentagon budget is slated to grow so much in coming years. Some of the upward pressure arises from high-profile issues such as missile defense, but most comes from the main combat systems of the military services, which are generally wearing out. Living off the fruits of the Reagan military buildup, the Clinton administration spent an average of $50 billion a year on equipment, only about 15 percent of the defense budget; in contrast, the historical average is about 25 percent. This "procurement holiday" is now ending, as it must.

Nevertheless, the Pentagon's weapons modernization plan is excessive. Despite President Bush's campaign promise in 1999–2000 to "skip a generation" of weaponry, his Pentagon has canceled only three major weapons systems—the Navy's lower-altitude missile defense program; the Army's Crusader howitzer, which was not especially expensive; and more recently the Army's Comanche helicopter. Although procurement budgets must continue rising, the rapid increases envisioned in current plans are not essential. Economies can almost certainly be found by expanding the application of modestly priced technologies, such as the precision weapons, unmanned vehicles, and communications systems used so effectively in Afghanistan and Iraq.

Like those of its predecessors, the Bush administration weapons modernization plan lacks clear priorities. It proposes to replace major combat systems throughout the force structure with systems typically costing twice as much. Simpler systems often will do. Even though procurement budgets have not yet risen dramatically, the current plan will soon oblige them to do so. It has already led to historic and huge increases in the RDT&E budget for advanced systems development, above and beyond high-profile missile defense programs. That budget was about $50 billion a year in the late cold war years and about $40 billion annually in the mid- to late 1990s. Today it is about $65 billion (all these figures are in constant 2005 dollars).[36]

A more discriminating and economy-minded modernization strategy would equip only part—not most or all—of the armed forces with extremely sophisticated and expensive weaponry. That high-end component would hedge against new possibilities, such as unexpectedly rapid modernizing of the Chinese armed forces. The rest of the U.S. military establishment would be equipped primarily with relatively inexpensive upgrades of existing weaponry, including better sensors, munitions, computers, and communications systems. This approach would also envision, over the longer term, greater use of unmanned platforms and other new concepts and capabilities, while being patient about when to deploy them. Such an approach would not keep the procurement budget in the current range of $70 billion to $75 billion, but it might hold it to $80 billion to $90 billion a year instead of the $100 billion or more now projected.

Privatization and Reform

All defense planners endeavor to save money in the relatively low-profile parts of the Pentagon budget known as operations and maintenance accounts. These accounts, which fund a wide range of activities including training, overseas deployments, upkeep of equipment, military base operations, and health care costs—in short, near-term military readiness—have been rising fast in recent years, and it will be hard to stop the upward trend.[37]

Some savings are already in the works. Congress has agreed to authorize another round of base closures in 2005.[38] Since the cold war ended, U.S. military forces have shrunk by more than one-third, yet domestic base capacity has fallen only 20 percent. That suggests that another reduction of 12 to 15 percent might be appropriate. The recent Bush administration decision to bring about 70,000 troops home from abroad might reduce the scale of the next BRAC (base realignment and closure) round, implying a net reduction closer to 10 percent of existing domestic capacity. But after initial implementation costs that could reach $10 billion or somewhat more, retrenchment of base capacity reportedly will save about $7 billion annually, including some savings from abroad.[39]

Overhauling military health care services by merging the independent health plans of each branch of military service and introducing a small copayment for military personnel and their families could save $2 billion per year.[40] Other savings in operations and maintenance are possible. For example, encouraging local base commanders to economize by letting them keep some of the savings for their base activities could save $1 billion a year or more within a decade.[41]

All that said, the activities funded by these accounts are crucial to national security and have proved tough to cap or contain. Privatization is no panacea; it takes time, sometimes raises complicated issues about deploying civilians to wartime environments, and generally saves much less than its warmest advocates claim.[42] Often it leads to increases in the size of the civilian personnel payroll funded out of the defense budget without reducing uniformed personnel—thereby potentially increasing, not reducing, total costs.

Another broad approach is to improve efficiency in employing and deploying military forces, which could lead to some cuts in personnel, at least over time. The Navy has some of the most interesting ideas on this, and they can be pursued further, perhaps allowing a modest decrease in the size of the fleet (in addition to reducing the strain on people and equipment). For example, more ships can be based near the regions where they are used, as with attack submarines on Guam. Crews can be airlifted from the United States to relieve other crews on ships deployed abroad, rather than sailing the ships all the way back to the United States so frequently. And the Navy's innovative concept for "surging" carriers from U.S. ports to hotspots during crises (or for exercises or other purposes)—instead of slavishly maintaining a constant presence in key overseas theaters—also could offer at least modest benefits.[43]

These cost-saving ideas all require further development. In particular, methods to reduce the cost of new weapons are discussed in chapter 5.

More Burden Sharing?

Today the United States outspends its major allies by about 2 to 1, but it outdistances them in military force that can be projected overseas and sustained there by a ratio of at least 5 to 1. Most American allies spent the cold war preparing to defend their own or nearby territories against a Soviet threat. American forces focused on how to deploy and operate forces many thousands of miles from home. Most U.S. allies have gotten serious about this effort only since the cold war ended (if then).

Shifting defense responsibilities to U.S. allies is an idea that is attractive in the United States. Unfortunately, the near-term prospects for doing so to any significant extent are not good, even though many U.S. allies have good militaries, strong military traditions, and a high-tech industrial base. The problem is largely political. It is not that Europeans are as force-averse as some argue. The claim that "Americans are from Mars, Europeans from Venus," meaning that the former are inclined to use force and the latter to use more peaceful inducements in their foreign policy, is overstated—as evidenced by European military action in Bosnia, Kosovo, Afghanistan, Africa, and to some extent even Iraq. However, it is probably true that Europeans do not believe the world to be quite as dangerous a place as Americans typically do. Several European countries face fiscal deficits that combined with their political priorities and their voters' perceptions of threat probably preclude big defense buildups. They also have strong incentives to free-ride, at least somewhat, on U.S. commitments and capabilities. On the other hand, European nations often cite their substantial contributions to peacekeeping missions as evidence that they are already bearing a considerable share of the defense burden. Germany and Japan are disinclined to remilitarize, and many of their former adversaries who vividly remember World War II hesitate to urge them to abandon their reticence.[44]

Some progress has been made. European militaries are developing the combined capacity to deploy up to 60,000 troops at a considerable geographic distance and to sustain them there for a year. Japan is slowly enlarging its interpretation of which military missions are consistent with its post–World War II constitution. U.S., British, and French programs are slowly helping African militaries improve their skills. And the recent transatlantic quarrel over Iraq may help motivate European countries to develop more military capability to gain greater influence in global decisions on the use of force.

But much more is needed. And much more is possible. Reallocations of about 10 percent of current allied military spending could, even without increased defense budgets, give other Organization for Economic Cooperation and Development (OECD) countries fully half as much deployable military capability as the United States within a decade.[45] That in turn could allow modest reductions in American troop strength—if not right away, then eventually.

Reductions in U.S. forces could never be as great as increases in allied forces, since there is no assurance that the latter would be available in large numbers in a given operation. But there are nonetheless benefits to greater allied capabilities. Even the Iraq stabilization effort, as unpopular as it has been, has seen an allied contribution of 15 percent of total forces—probably a floor below which future contributions would rarely if ever drop. More often, with better diplomacy than employed by the Bush administration on Iraq policy, it should be realistic to expect allied assistance in the range of at least 25 percent of a given operation's total strength. Levels could reach 50 percent or more in operations near Europe (as in the Balkans, where Europeans have typically provided 75 percent of the total). So a larger pool of capable forces from friendly countries would help the United States—eventually.

Growing the Ground Forces

The case for increasing expenditures in one part of the defense budget—the size and cost of ground forces—also needs to be made. Enormous strain is now being imposed on U.S. soldiers and Marines by the Iraq mission and other responsibilities. The Rumsfeld Pentagon has pursued a number of approaches to free up more soldiers and Marines for deployment out of those already in the armed forces. But those initiatives, while worthy and indeed bold, are not enough given the demands of the times, as argued at greater length in chapter 3.

The United States should promptly increase the number of combat soldiers and Marines by a total of roughly 40,000 active duty troops—and perhaps more depending on future events—beyond the increase of some 25,000 that the Bush administration has already carried out. Today's operations, which could last several more years, are too much for the all-volunteer force to be expected to sustain at its current size. Indeed, an increase is already eighteen months overdue. Even though it could take two to three years to carry out fully, it must begin—even if there is a chance that the Iraq operation will be terminated or substantially downsized while the increase is being put into effect. The cost of modestly and temporarily increasing the size of the U.S. ground forces, while large, is not terribly onerous. By contrast, the consequences for the nation of continuing to overdeploy soldiers and Marines and thereby risking a rapidly intensifying personnel shortage would be enormous. It is not necessary to run that risk.

Over the longer term, even after the Iraq and Afghanistan missions are completed, the United States will still need substantial ground forces, in addition to major naval and air capabilities. In all likelihood, a force structure similar in size to today's will be needed then, though it may eventually be possible to reduce personnel rosters by 5 to 10 percent. The types of future scenarios that could require these forces are sketched in chapter 6. But for now, the pressure of current operations is what must concern American defense planners most—and that pressure requires a temporary increase, not a decrease, in Army and Marine Corps personnel.

TWO   # Setting the Context:
The Afghanistan and Iraq Wars
and Their Lessons

Wars in general always teach a great deal about military operations. Because the recent wars in Afghanistan and Iraq have also helped establish the circumstances in which American armed forces now find themselves around the world, these wars in particular should be reviewed before developing recommendations about the future.

The most important single question is this: did Operation Enduring Freedom and Operation Iraqi Freedom validate a new theory of warfare according to which special forces, high technology, and creative war plans will replace America's traditional assets of firepower, maneuver, and brute strength? If so, the implications for defense planning could be sweeping.

That is a quite dubious proposition, however. It comes closer to being true in Afghanistan, though even there the presence of substantial numbers of local allies was critical to defeating the Taliban and al Qaeda. And in Iraq, even leaving aside the demands of the post-Saddam stabilization mission, traditional combat capabilities mattered a great deal in the intensive invasion phase of the war.

Those who would jettison the Powell doctrine of overwhelming force in favor of a Rumsfeld doctrine of stealth, surprise, finesse, and small coalitions of the willing should therefore temper their views.[1] Rumsfeld's thinking about how to use precision and speed to win battlefield victories is provocative and useful. But the tasks of the U.S. military go well beyond achieving traditional battlefield victories, and sometimes winning even traditional victories requires lots of brute strength. That being the case, the United States must retain a broad range of capabilities, including substantial ground forces—capabilities that will, as discussed further in chapter 6, be necessary even after the Iraq and Afghanistan missions are completed.

That said, the opportunities offered to the military by modern electronics, communications, unmanned vehicles, and systems integration are considerable. They do indeed afford a means of substantially improving defense capabilities at relatively modest cost; in fact, that has been true for some time now. That point reinforces the general message of chapter 5—that there are prudent ways to trim planned purchases of expensive weapons platforms, such as next-generation fighter jets and submarines, and save money in the process. The savings are not great enough to permit reductions in the defense budget, or even to preclude the need for further real-dollar increases. But they can help pay for the increases in troop strength that are so clearly needed.

Operation Enduring Freedom

The U.S. forces involved in the Afghanistan war effort numbered no more than 60,000, about half of which were in the Persian Gulf. Western allies added no more than 15,000. But the U.S.-led military campaign was hardly small in scale. By the end of January 2002, the United States had flown about 25,000 sorties in the air campaign and dropped 18,000 bombs, including 10,000 precision munitions. The number of U.S. sorties exceeded the number the United States flew in the 1999 Kosovo war, and the United States dropped more smart bombs on Afghanistan than NATO dropped on Serbia in 1999. In fact, the total number of precision munitions expended by then in Afghanistan amounted to more than half the number used in Operation Desert Storm. In addition, more than 3,000 U.S. and French bombs were dropped on surviving enemy forces in March 2002 during Operation Anaconda, in which some 1,500 Western forces and 2,000 Afghans launched a major offensive against about 1,000 enemy troops in the mountainous region of eastern Afghanistan.[2]

Beginning on October 7, 2001, Afghans, Americans, and coalition partners cooperated to produce a remarkable military victory against the

Taliban and al Qaeda in Afghanistan. Contributing to that victory were 15,000 Northern Alliance fighters (primarily from the Tajik and Uzbek ethnic groups), 100 combat sorties a day by U.S. planes, 300 to 500 Western special operations forces and intelligence operatives, a few thousand Western ground forces, and thousands of Pashtun soldiers in southern Afghanistan who came over to the winning side in November. Together they defeated the Taliban forces, estimated at 50,000 to 60,000 strong, as well as a few thousand al Qaeda fighters.[3]

Various Western countries, particularly several NATO allies and Australia, played important roles as well. A formal NATO role in the war was neither necessary nor desirable, given the location of the conflict and the need for a supple and secretive military strategy. Still, after September 11 NATO allies—invoking Article V, the alliance's mutual-defense clause— stood squarely by America's side and demonstrated their commitment by sending five AWACS aircraft to help patrol U.S. airspace. Forces from the United Kingdom, Australia, France, and Canada contributed frequently to the effort in Afghanistan, and forces from Denmark, Norway, and Germany also participated in Operation Anaconda in March. Allied aircraft flew a total of some 3,000 sorties on relief, reconnaissance, and other missions. As noted, France dropped bombs during Operation Anaconda, and the United Kingdom fired several cruise missiles on the first day of battle as well. Numerous countries, including the Netherlands, Italy, and Japan, deployed ships to the Arabian Sea. Cooperation continues today, as major Western allies constitute the backbone of the UN-authorized stabilization force in Kabul.

During phase one, the first month or so of the war, Taliban forces lost their major physical assets, such as radar, aircraft, and command-and-control systems, but they hung on to power in most regions. Most al Qaeda training camps and headquarters also were destroyed. Although Taliban forces did not quickly collapse, they were increasingly isolated in pockets near large cities. Cut off from each other physically, they were unable to resupply or reinforce themselves very well and had problems communicating effectively.

In the first week of the war, U.S. aircraft averaged only twenty-five combat sorties a day, but that total was soon upped to around 100. Some seventy Tomahawk cruise missiles were fired in the early going; a total of about 100 had been used by December 2001. The number of airlift, refueling, and other support missions saw a comparable increase. U.S. air strikes by B-52 and B-1 bombers operating out of the British island territory of Diego Garcia typically involved six sorties a day; other land-based aircraft, primarily F-15Es and AC-130 gunships from Oman, flew about as much. Planes from the three U.S. aircraft carriers based in the Arabian Sea provided the rest of the air combat punch. Reconnaissance and refueling flights originated in the Persian Gulf region and in Diego Garcia, in the Indian Ocean. Some air support and relief missions also came from or flew over Central Asia, where U.S. soldiers from the 10th Mountain Division helped protect airfields.

Most air attacks occurred around Afghanistan's perimeter, because the rugged central highlands were not a major operating area for the Taliban or al Qaeda. By the middle of October 2001, most fixed assets worth striking had already been hit, so combat sorties turned to targeting Taliban and al Qaeda forces in the field. Aircraft continued to fly at an altitude of at least 10,000 feet, because the Pentagon was fearful of anti-aircraft artillery, Soviet SA-7 and SA-13 portable anti-aircraft missiles, and some 200 to 300 Stinger anti-aircraft missiles presumed to be in Taliban or al Qaeda possession. But most precision-guided weapons are equally effective regardless of their altitude of origin, provided that good targeting information is available—as it was in this case, thanks to U.S. personnel and Afghan allies on the ground.

In phase two, beginning in early November, the air campaign intensified, due not so much to an increase in the number of airplanes as to an increase in their effectiveness. By then, 80 percent of U.S. combat sorties could be devoted to directly supporting Afghan opposition forces in the field; by late November, the tally was 90 percent. In addition, the deployment of more unmanned aerial vehicles and JSTARS (joint surveillance and target attack radar system) aircraft to the region helped the United States maintain continuous reconnaissance of enemy forces in many areas. Most important, the number of U.S. special operations forces and CIA teams working with various Afghan opposition elements increased greatly. In mid-October, only three special operations "A teams," each consisting of a dozen personnel, were in Afghanistan; in mid-November, there were ten; by December 8, there were seventeen. That change meant that the

United States could increasingly call in supplies for the Afghan opposition forces, help them with tactics, and designate Taliban and al Qaeda targets for U.S. air strikes by using global positioning system (GPS) technology and laser range finders. The Marine Corps also began to provide logistical support for these teams as the war advanced. And the Afghan opposition forces performed more effectively as well.[4]

As a result, enemy forces collapsed in northern cities such as Mazar-i-Sharif and Taloqan over the weekend of November 9. By November 16, Pentagon officials were estimating that the Taliban controlled less than one-third of the country, in contrast to 85 percent just a week before. Muhammad Atef, a key al Qaeda operative, was killed during U.S. bombing in mid-November. Kunduz, the last northern stronghold of enemy forces, where several thousand Taliban and al Qaeda troops apparently remained, fell on November 25.

In late November, more than 1,000 U.S. Marines of the 15th and the 26th Marine Expeditionary Units established a base about sixty miles southwest of Kandahar, which the Taliban continued to hold. They deployed there directly from ships in the Arabian Sea, leapfrogging over Pakistani territory at night (to minimize political difficulties for the government of President Pervez Musharraf) and flying 400 miles inland to what became known as Camp Rhino. Subsequent resupply missions were largely conducted using Pakistani bases. Once deployed, the Marines began to interdict some road traffic and carry out support missions for special operations forces.

Meanwhile, members of the Pashtun ethnic group had begun to oppose the Taliban openly. By November, they were accepting the help of U.S. special forces, who had previously been active principally in the north of the country. Two groups in particular—one led by Hamid Karzai, the other by another tribal leader, Gul Agha Shirzai—closed in on Kandahar. Mullah Omar offered to surrender in early December but in the end fled with most of his fighters, leaving the city open by December 9. Pockets of Taliban and al Qaeda resistance, each with hundreds of fighters or more, remained in areas near Mazar-i-Sharif, Kabul, Kandahar, and possibly elsewhere, but the Taliban no longer held cities or major transportation routes. And those pockets of fighters could be attacked by coalition forces.

The third main phase of the war began in early December 2001. By this time, U.S. intelligence had pinpointed much of the al Qaeda force near Jalalabad, in eastern Afghanistan, and Osama bin Laden and his contingent in particular were thought to have holed up in the mountain redoubts of Tora Bora. Earlier, on November 29, Vice President Dick Cheney had confirmed the intelligence, telling Diane Sawyer of ABC News, "I think he's probably in that general area."[5] Traveling with perhaps 1,000 to 2,000 foreign fighters, most of them fellow Arabs, bin Laden could not easily evade detection by curious eyes even if he might elude U.S. overhead reconnaissance. Therefore, once Afghan opposition fighters, together with CIA and special operations forces, were deployed in the vicinity, U.S. air strikes against the caves could become quite effective. By mid-December, the fight for Tora Bora was over. Most significant cave openings were destroyed and virtually all signs of live al Qaeda fighters disappeared. Sporadic bombing continued in the area, and it was not until mid-January 2002 that a major al Qaeda training base, Zawar Kili, was destroyed. But most bombing ended by late 2001.

So why did bin Laden and other top al Qaeda leaders get away? The United States relied too much on Pakistan and its Afghan allies to close off possible escape routes from the Tora Bora region, and they may not have had the same incentives as the United States to conduct the effort with dogged persistence. Admittedly, there were reasons not to put many Americans in Afghanistan. First, Washington feared a possible anti-American backlash, as Rumsfeld made clear in public comments. Complicating matters, the United States would have had a hard time getting several thousands of troops into Afghanistan, since no neighboring country except Pakistan would have been a viable staging base and Pakistan was not willing to play that role. Putting several thousand U.S. forces in that mountainous inland region would have been difficult and dangerous. Yet given the enormous stakes in this war, it would have been appropriate; indeed, CENTCOM made preparations for doing so. But in the end, partly because of logistical challenges but perhaps partly because of the Pentagon's aversion to U.S. casualties, the idea was dropped.

What would have been needed for the United States to perform this mission? To close off the 100 to 150 escape routes along the twenty-five-mile stretch of the Afghan-Pakistani border closest to Tora Bora would have required perhaps 1,000 to 3,000 American troops. Deploying such a force from the United States would have required several hundred airlifts, followed by ferrying the troops and supplies to frontline positions by helicopter. According to CENTCOM, creating a new airfield might have been necessary, largely to deliver fuel. Such an operation would have taken a week or more. But two Marine Corps units with more than 1,000 personnel were already in the country in December and were somewhat idle at that time. If redeployed to Tora Bora, they could have helped prevent al Qaeda's escape themselves. They also could have been reinforced over subsequent days and weeks by Army light forces or more Marines, who could have closed off possible escape routes into the interior of Afghanistan. Such an effort would not have ensured success, but the odds would have favored the United States.

So the Afghan conflict, while truly pathbreaking in its use of high-tech weapons such as GPS-guided bombs and Predator unmanned aerial vehicles as well as special forces, did not invalidate past concepts of warfare altogether. The Northern Alliance and other Afghan units were needed on the ground to help defeat the Taliban and al Qaeda. In addition, U.S. forces failed to achieve key objectives in and around Tora Bora by relying too much on airpower and local allies. Finally, stabilizing Afghanistan effectively would have required considerably more forces—if not during main combat operations, then after. So advocates of military revolution and rapid transformation need to temper any claims that Operation Enduring Freedom proves a case for radical change.[6]

Operation Iraqi Freedom

American, British, and Australian forces accomplished a remarkable feat between March 19 and April 9, 2003, roughly the period of the main combat operations in Iraq. They defeated a 400,000-man military, overthrew a dictator, and successfully conducted major urban combat operations while suffering fewer than 200 combat deaths—even smaller coalition losses than in Operation Desert Storm a decade ago.

What was responsible for this remarkable battlefield success? Were Vice President Dick Cheney and Richard Myers, chairman of the Joint Chiefs of Staff, right when they claimed that the strategy devised by General Tommy Franks and his colleagues at CENTCOM was brilliant? Will war colleges around the world be teaching that strategy to their students decades from now? Or will the conflict tend to be seen primarily as a case of overwhelming military capability prevailing over a mediocre army from a mid-sized developing country?

Despite the claims of some observers during and right after the war, whether the military strategy used in Iraq deserves to be called brilliant is debatable. On balance, U.S. military performance was so good and U.S. military supremacy so overwhelming that the American-led coalition probably could have won the war fast without a brilliant war plan or even a very good one. That said, there were major elements of military creativity in the Iraq campaign, as well as some that were nothing new. Consider several key elements:

—*Shock and awe.* This was, of course, the bumper sticker slogan for how the war would begin, well advertised weeks in advance. But the idea was not that new. Selectively hitting military targets while sparing civilian infrastructure is an idea that builds on the U.S. experience in Afghanistan, Kosovo, and Operation Desert Storm. Striking hard in the early hours of a war is a strategy that air power proponents have counseled for decades. In the end, the shock-and-awe concept was not really followed, because plans apparently changed with the attempt to kill Saddam on March 19. Given the degree to which Iraqi forces had become accustomed to coalition bombing in the preceding decade, there probably would not have been much shock or awe involved in any case.

—*Special operations raids.* These were more impressive than the early air campaign. Dozens of small special operations teams disrupted Iraqi command and control, seized oil infrastructure, prevented dams from being demolished, and took hold of airfields in regions where Scud missiles might have been launched at Israel. Special operations and intelligence units also appear to have disrupted Iraqi lines of communication in Baghdad and elsewhere, perhaps hastening the collapse of Iraqi forces once the urban fighting began. These operations were done in a brave, creative, and effective manner. They also prevented some nightmarish scenarios. And in several places in the north and west of Iraq, small teams of special forces helped hold off much larger Iraqi main combat formations at key moments.[7]

—*Bypassing southeastern cities while rushing to Baghdad.* In the first ten days of the war, it was not clear that coalition ground forces could protect their flanks sufficiently in the areas that they preferred not to seize. The ensuing debate was somewhat overblown. In a worst case, coalition forces could have waited a couple of weeks for other units to arrive, and in all likelihood only modest harm would have been done to the broader strategy. (Admittedly, Saddam would have had more time to consider steps like blowing up dams or fortifying Baghdad in the event of such a delay, but he had some time to carry out these kinds of tactics even as events unfolded and made little use of it.) Regardless, this approach, which placed a premium on speed and deep penetration, was hardly new. Hitler's generals did not make pit stops in Strasbourg or Luxembourg or northeastern France; they drove straight for the French coast to cut off the French army, and for Paris. And a related aspect of the strategy, avoiding attacks against regular Iraqi military units (in the interest of targeting elite units and maximizing the speed of advance), was also smart. But it was well known that these forces were much less loyal to Saddam than were the Special Republican Guard, Republican Guard, and fedayeen units.

—*Powerful air bombardment of Iraqi forces.* The combination of GPS-guided all-weather bombs; better all-weather sensors, such as JSTARS aircraft flying well within Iraqi airspace; and real-time joint communications networks denied Iraqi forces any sanctuary. For the first time in combat, nine JSTARS aircraft were deployed to a war theater, allowing the United States to maintain three in the air continuously.[8] Air Force B-1 bombers were among the platforms performing especially well, in this case dropping almost half of all GPS-guided JDAMs (joint direct attack munitions) used in the war despite flying just 2 percent of total sorties. That shows the value of bombers and also that a great deal can be done with a modest number, at least when targets are relatively concentrated.[9] Even if the Iraqis tried to move during sandstorms or at night, coalition forces could see and strike them. In addition, due to the rapid movements of coalition ground forces, any Iraqi redeployments had to occur quickly if they were to help frontline forces under attack. That fact made it more likely that they would move in large formations on roadways, as they did, and they were badly hurt as a result. Again, that was textbook doctrine, applied with better technology than ever before, rather than brilliant strategizing.

—*Devastating combined arms attacks against the Republican Guard.*
In addition to the combat dynamics mentioned, coalition forces were
remarkably effective when air and ground units worked together. By the
last days of March and early days of April, U.S. Army and Marine Corps
forces were mauling Republican Guard troops deployed outside Baghdad. Saddam made a major mistake in keeping them there, perhaps out of
fear that they would turn against him if allowed into Baghdad or perhaps
out of overconfidence that they could hide in the complex terrain of the
Tigris-Euphrates Valley. The coalition did employ some creative tactics—
such as the 3rd Mechanized Infantry Division's "bump and run" move to
outflank part of the Madinah Division near Karbala—but what won the
fight was a devastating display of combined arms warfare. It built principally on a decades-old concept, adopted and integrated into U.S. military
doctrine and tactics during the Reagan, Bush, and Clinton years, combined with dramatically improved technology—for example, friendly-
force tracking systems such as FBCB2, which were installed on about 10
percent of all Army vehicles and reduced "fratricide" substantially.[10] There
were some aspects of the use of airpower on the country's periphery that
were more similar to tactics used in the Afghanistan campaign, in which
U.S. aircraft supported special forces on the ground. But in the main battles, what prevailed was less brilliance or radical new concepts of warfare
than sheer dominance in traditional combined arms operations, made
even more effective by new technology.

—*The fights for Baghdad and Basra.* Here, there was some genuine
cleverness and creativity. To try to seize the cities quickly probably would
have produced high casualties on all sides. In contrast, to wait patiently
for the 4th Mechanized Infantry Division and other reinforcements would
have given Saddam's forces time to regroup and devise new tactics. So the
middle ground—using increasingly assertive "reconnaissance in force"
operations to gain information, disrupt Saddam's forces, and engage selectively in firefights against elite Iraqi forces—was just right. The topography of Baghdad, with its wide boulevards, helped; the Iraqi fighters' dis-
organized and ineffectual efforts helped even more. So, as Center for
Strategic and International Studies scholar Anthony Cordesman under-
scores, one should not assume that future urban operations will be so
straightforward; indeed, the post-invasion experience in Iraq itself has

already taught that lesson. But a combination of American Army and Marine Corps infantry skills, the combat setting, and Iraqi fecklessness made for a quick, decisive urban fight.[11] The British were every bit as effective in Basra, using a similar type of approach—and in the aftermath of Saddam's fall, they have been on balance more effective in Basra than most U.S. forces have been elsewhere in the country.[12]

Overall, the main pillars of the coalition's success in Iraq—new technology and traditional skills—made for a remarkable set of capabilities. In terms of equipment, of particular note were the all-weather reconnaissance systems, all-weather bombs, and modern communications networks developed in the last decade. (These new capabilities appeared during a period when, ironically, advocates of defense revolution were often frustrated at the pace of change in the U.S. armed forces.) Also impressive was the global transportation capability used to deploy forces to the theater quickly, even if the process of computerizing and tagging shipments was still badly incomplete.[13] In particular, C-17 aircraft and LMSR fast sealift ships purchased during the Clinton administration performed quite effectively.[14] In addition, the competence of American and British troops and their commanders and the excellence of their training were striking. Indeed, old-fashioned equipment such as tanks performed extremely well, the old-fashioned skills of infantry soldiers were very important, and overall the urban combat operations were executed magnificently.

The main issues requiring remedial action on the part of the U.S. military concern the post-Saddam period. At this point, the single most glaring problem has become the strain on the U.S. Army and Marine Corps in particular resulting from a prolonged and difficult operation that could last for years. Part of the problem, notably the lack of preparation for the post-Saddam period and the loss of control that followed, reflected poor performance on the part of the Department of Defense after a remarkably successful invasion. (Another issue, whether the United States needs dedicated forces for peacekeeping and stabilization missions, is addressed in chapter 4.)

Secretary Rumsfeld—who was the primary proponent of using a small force and who more than anyone insisted on assuming that post-Saddam Iraq would present a benign environment—must accept most of the responsibility. But the uniformed military planners who were prepared to accept that assumption share the blame. Some military planners reportedly did investigate the requirements of the post-Saddam environment in detail, and some may have spoken of their broad findings to the secretary of defense. However, it appears that they were too quick to give up the effort once their initial suggestions met resistance. According to what information can be gleaned from the outside, their work did not wind up in the official war plans—or even in any unofficial, backup plans that it would have been prudent to develop, with or without the formal blessing of the secretary of defense. Indeed, the Army's official history of the war reveals that, despite planning very carefully and rigorously for the invasion operation, the Army barely considered the post-invasion environment itself.

Optimistic assumptions that the conventional Iraqi military forces would not resist for long proved largely right. But optimistic assumptions that they and other elements of the Iraqi security services would therefore quickly become available to help stabilize the country proved badly wrong.[15] So, therefore, did administration expectations that initial U.S. troop levels in Iraq could be cut by 50,000 within three months and by another 50,000 shortly thereafter, with virtually all coming home within the first year.[16]

It is indefensible to undertake regime change without planning on a difficult postconflict environment, which many had predicted before the war began. It is difficult to assess how much the mistakes made early on in the post-Saddam period have contributed to the difficult environment that persists today, but they undoubtedly played a role, breeding cynicism among the Iraqi population about the intent of U.S.-led forces and allowing insurgents to regroup and recover.[17] The next chapter wrestles with the challenge this situation presents to today's all-volunteer military.

THREE The Need to Increase the Size of U.S. Ground Forces

After criticizing the Clinton administration for overdeploying and overusing the U.S. military in the 1990s, President Bush and his administration did exactly the same thing—but on a much larger scale. That observation is not a criticism of the decision to overthrow Saddam Hussein. But having made the decision—and having badly underestimated the forces needed to stabilize Iraq after Saddam was overthrown as well as the difficulty of doing so—the Bush administration left the U.S. ground forces too small to meet the ensuing challenges successfully.

The problem is most acute for the U.S. Army, which numbers only a half-million active duty troops (see table 3-1), and the 175,000-strong U.S. Marine Corps. Most Navy and Air Force personnel involved in the invasion went home to a grateful nation after Saddam was overthrown. The strains that the Iraqi no-fly-zones caused on many types of Air Force and Navy assets and personnel are now gone as well. Certain Air Force aircraft, notably tankers and transports, admittedly continue to work very hard to support the Afghanistan and Iraq operations—perhaps at twice the frequency of missions of several years ago.[1] But the strain has shifted away from the tactical combat forces, and in any case Navy and Air Force efforts involve no more than about 20,000 personnel at a time.[2]

Moreover, both the Air Force and Navy have adopted new patterns of operations that have further eased the burden on personnel. The Air Force

Table 3-1. *Existing and Planned Active Duty Force Levels*[a]

Service	Authorized (09/03)	Actual (09/03)	Mobilized reserves (09/03)	Bush 2005 request (02/04)	Authorized FY 2005
Army	480.0	499.3	127.5	482.4	502.0/532.0[b]
Marine Corps	175.0	177.8	11.1	175.0	178.0/187.0[b]
Navy	375.7	382.2	3.5	368.1	365.9
Air Force	359.0	375.1	21.2	359.8	359.7

Sources: Under Secretary of Defense David Chu, "How Might We Think about Stress on the Force?" Briefing at the Pentagon, February 11, 2004; and U.S. House of Representatives, "Conference Report to Accompany H.R. 4200, the Ronald W. Reagan National Defense Authorization Act for Fiscal Year 2005," October 8, 2004 (www.house.gov/rules/1084200confrept.pdf [October 22, 2004]).

a. Thousands of personnel.

b. The Congress gave the secretary of defense authority to exceed the 2005 minimum force levels for the Army and Marine Corps (502,000 and 178,000 respectively) by 30,000 soldiers and 9,000 Marines.

has organized itself into Air Expeditionary Forces—essentially on-call packages of several types of capabilities that take turns being ready to deploy quickly if needed.[3] And the Navy has reduced somewhat its emphasis on maintaining a continuous overseas presence (largely due, it appears, to the improved security environment in the Persian Gulf) in favor of maintaining more carriers ready to deploy quickly if a crisis erupts.[4]

In contrast, the Army still has nearly 150,000 troops deployed in and around Iraq, and some 15,000 more are in Afghanistan. In addition, it has more than 20,000 in Korea, 2,000 in the Balkans, and dozens here and hundreds there on temporary assignments around the world. Virtually all of these soldiers, the majority of them married, are currently separated from their home bases and families. Marines are now bearing much of the brunt of U.S. security missions as well, having again deployed forces to Iraq and elsewhere. The Pentagon has made a number of temporary changes in policy to relieve the strain somewhat, such as canceling more than a quarter of its training exercises, but enormous strain remains nonetheless.[5]

Fortunately, in recent years all branches of the armed services have met most of their recruiting and retention goals.[6] That continued to be true through the end of fiscal year 2004,[7] but initial data for fiscal year 2005 show that results have been less than excellent. Also, some standards, such as the number of non–high school graduates accepted into the military, had to be softened to meet 2004 goals. But none of these issues is likely in and of itself to be serious; on balance, recruiting and retention efforts were holding up passably well as of early 2005.[8] Indeed, the Air Force is retaining active duty personnel quite well, at a rate better than recent historical averages, and it has had to reduce its recruiting targets for the next two or three years to accomplish a modest downsizing of the force.[9]

That is not cause for complacency, however, especially for U.S. ground forces. For one thing, so-called stop-loss orders have prevented many soldiers from leaving the military—at least 24,000 active duty troops and 16,000 reservists through early 2004.[10] For another, the fact that the Army will have to continue to deploy and redeploy forces abroad is only now becoming well known around the country. The surge of patriotism after 9/11, the impressive successes of the U.S. military in toppling the Taliban and Saddam Hussein, and improved military compensation have helped prevent a "hollowing out" of the military to date. But it would be irresponsible to assume that that state of affairs will continue.

Indeed, there are serious warning signs on the horizon, including an early 2004 *Washington Post* poll that indicated that three-fourths of all Army spouses expected the service to face reenlistment problems in the coming months, as well as surveys of troops in Iraq indicating some serious morale issues.[11] Rather than allow recruits the normal period of several months between commitment to enlist and commencement of service, the Army has had to quickly enlist several thousand more recruits from the so-called delayed entry program. The Army National Guard was several thousand individuals behind in its recruiting goals for 2004, and both it and the Army Reserve were experiencing significant shortfalls in early 2005.[12] The Army has also had to call up more than 5,000 reservists from the individual ready reserve (individuals who are not part of any formal formations). This is not an unreasonable action to take in times of severe strain on the force. Similarly, the Army's decisions to send one of two brigades normally stationed in Korea to Iraq—and also to deploy elements of the "opposition force" units, which traditionally help train other combat forces, from national training centers to Iraq—are acceptable given the circumstances. But the fact that such measures are now necessary should alert the nation's leaders to the nature of the current situation.[13]

As things stand, the typical active duty U.S. soldier in a deployable unit could spend literally the majority of the next three to four years abroad. A majority of the units deploying to Iraq in late 2004 and thereafter are going for the second time.[14] In 2004 alone, twenty-six of the Army's thirty-three main combat brigades in the active force deployed abroad at some point; over the course of 2003 and 2004 together, virtually all of the thirty-three brigades were deployed (see table 3-2).

When units deploy more than once in a short space of time, not everyone within those units deploys more than once. Typical personnel turnover in a given military unit runs about 50 percent a year. Still, roughly half of all individuals in a given unit could deploy more than once if the unit is sent overseas again after a short stint at home, and some individuals could wind up being deployed a second time with a different unit.[15]

The typical reservist might be deployed for another twelve months over the next three to four years. As one example, all fifteen of the Army National Guard's enhanced separate brigades are to be deployed at some point by 2006,[16] but the greatest problem is with units that have to be mobilized more than once.[17]

The overall rate of Army overseas deployments away from home base (and families) is more than twice what it was during the 1990s, when overdeployment was frequently blamed for shortfalls in meeting recruiting and retention goals.[18] So history suggests that current operations could pose a major challenge to the force.

The United States cannot at this point realistically expect a great deal more help from its allies, given the strong opposition of many of them to its mission in Iraq. It might be more productive to try to persuade France and Germany to add several thousand soldiers in Afghanistan; at present, NATO is falling short of its goal of maintaining just 10,000 troops there. However, in a country like Afghanistan (with the size and population of Iraq), the proper goal would be at least 20,000 troops. The meager effort in Afghanistan is occurring despite President Bush's promise in November of 2001 that "America will join the world in helping the people of Afghanistan rebuild their country . . . and the United States will work with the U.N. to support a post-Taliban government that represents all of the Afghan people." At present it is hard to believe that the task is being accomplished when most of Afghanistan is beyond the control of President

Table 3-2. *Recent Deployments of Army Active Duty Combat Units through Mid-2004*[a]

Unit	Deployment in 2003–04	Brigades deployed
3rd Infantry Division (Georgia)	Iraq (Rotation 1)	3
101st Airborne Division (Kentucky)	Iraq (Rotation 1)	3
4th Infantry Division (Texas)	Iraq (Rotation 1)	3
173rd Airborne Brigade (Italy)	Iraq (Rotation 1)	1
3rd Armored Cavalry Regiment (Colorado)	Iraq (Rotation 1)	1
1st Armored Division (Germany)	Iraq ("Rotation 1.5")	3
2nd Armored Cavalry Regiment (Louisiana)	Iraq ("Rotation 1.5")	1
1st Infantry Division (Germany)	Iraq (Rotation 2)	3
2nd Infantry Division, Stryker (Washington)	Iraq (Rotation 2)	1
25th Infantry Division (Hawaii)	Iraq (Rotation 2)	1
1st Cavalry Division (Texas)	Iraq (Rotation 2)	3
82nd Airborne Division (North Carolina)	Iraq (Rotation 2)	1
82nd Airborne Division (North Carolina)	Afghanistan (Rotation 2)	1
10th Mountain Division (New York)	Afghanistan (Rotations 1 and 2)	2 (x 2 deployments)
25th Infantry Division (Hawaii)	Afghanistan (Rotation 3)	2
2nd Infantry Division (Korea)	Korea (long-standing)	2 (x 2 deployments)
Total		34

Source: Bradley Graham, "Huge Movement of Troops Is Underway," *Washington Post*, January 9, 2004, p. A13; "National Guard and the Enhanced Brigades" (www.army.mil/soldiers/jan2002/pdfs/divisions.pdf); and R. L. Brownlee and General Peter J. Schoomaker, *Posture of the United States Army 2004* (U.S. Army, February 5, 2004), p. 9.

a. The 1st Marine Division has also deployed to Iraq twice, during the invasion and in 2004, and it was replaced by the 2nd Marine Division in the fall of 2004. From its National Guard forces, the Army also deployed the 53rd enhanced separate brigade (Florida) and the 76th enhanced separate brigade (Indiana) to Iraq in the first post-Saddam deployment, followed by the 30th enhanced separate brigade (North Carolina), the 81st enhanced separate brigade (Washington state), and the 39th enhanced separate brigade (Arkansas) in 2004. In all, five of fifteen enhanced separate brigades deployed in 2003, and six were deployed in 2004.

Karzai, who in the summer of 2004 gave the overall state of his country the grade of "D."[19]

Restructuring and Rebalancing the Total Army

Before estimating how many additional soldiers and Marines are required in today's armed forces, it is important to ask whether there are more efficient ways to structure and use them. Indeed, such an effort is under way.

Under the able guidance of Army Chief of Staff Peter Schoomaker and Secretary of Defense Rumsfeld, the Army has embarked on an ambitious plan to reassign many of its personnel over the course of the rest of the decade. Units of less likely utility on the modern battlefield will in many cases be eliminated to permit increases in those units that have been in highest demand in recent years and that seem likely to remain heavily employed in the future. In addition, the Army is now converting some 10,000 military jobs to civilian positions annually, freeing soldiers for high-demand tasks.[20] This idea, while bold, is not entirely new or radical. Even in the late 1990s, the Army's own war plans suggested that it had 150,000 too many combat troops (mostly in the National Guard) and 50,000 too few support troops, suggesting that there was a strong case then for a major overhaul to rebalance them.[21]

Under the new plan, the Army will streamline its field artillery, air defense, engineer, and armor units substantially, reducing them by twenty-four, ten, eleven, and nineteen battalions, respectively. It will reassign many of the billets to augment specialties such as transportation, civil affairs, military police, and other commonly used units.[22]

Special operations forces are being expanded as well. Numbers will increase in civil affairs and psychological operations units as well as commando teams and other combat formations. Currently, the Special Operations Command has jurisdiction over some 35,000 active duty troops (though as table 3-3 indicates, only a few thousand of them are special forces of the combat variety). Overall special operations forces will increase substantially—probably by several thousand—under the administration's plan. (An increase of 1,400 has been requested for 2006.) That idea makes sense; for example, existing capabilities were not adequate for conducting robust missions in Afghanistan and Iraq at the same time.[23]

That said, expanding special operations forces must be done carefully. Unusual skills are required for most such jobs, and it is not clear that the military can attract large additional numbers of the right types of people. The demands on individuals are great, as reflected in dropout rates in training, which are upward of 50 percent for many types of special operations units.[24] With special forces, sacrificing quality for quantity would be especially ill-advised.[25]

Table 3-3. *Army Force Structure (thousands of troops)*[a]

Specialty	Active troops	Reserve personnel	Total	Planned changes
Main specialties				
Air Defense Artillery	12	9	21	Reduction
Armor	24	29	53	Reduction
Artillery	29	48	77	Reduction
Aviation	25	21	46	
Engineering	21	62	83	Reduction
Infantry	49	57	106	
Maintenance	10	33	43	
Military Intelligence	24	13	37	Increase
Military Police	16	27	43	Increase
Signal (Communications)	22	16	38	
Transportation	12	41	53	Increase
Subtotal	234	356	590	
Support and secondary specialties				
Adjutant General, Finance, Chaplain, History, Judge Advocate, Public Information	14	23	37	
Chemical	3	9	12	Increase
Civil Affairs	0.6	6	7	Increase
Combat Service Support (indirect support)	38	43	81	Increase
Medical	10	27	36	
Ordnance, Quartermaster, and Supply	11	32	43	Some increases; some reductions
Psychological Operations	1.2	2.2	3	Increase
Security	3	0	3	
Special Forces	8	4	12	Increase
Support for miscellaneous specific units	12	8	20	
Subtotal	101	154	255	
Grand Total	335	510	845	

Source: U.S. Army communication to author, 2003.

a. Figures are generally rounded to the nearest thousand. Many individuals in the Army total force, which numbers more than 1 million, are not shown here; these may include individuals in training, headquarters, acquisition, and other such positions.

Such units are at their most effective when deployments call for speed, stealth, and flexibility—attributes that are harder to inculcate and display in a larger organization than a smaller one. Given that the U.S. special forces as a group are already comparable in size to an entire traditional branch of military service of many U.S. allies—and several times their own size a quarter-century ago—any expansion should be carried out gradually. In fact, it should probably occur at roughly the rate currently intended by the Army.[26]

Besides special forces, certain other units are being affected by the Army's ongoing restructuring. The exact number of personnel to be shifted is unclear from existing documents, but the total is reported to exceed 100,000, or some 10 percent, of total Army uniformed personnel. Those specialties expected to undergo significant increases or reductions in troop totals are indicated in table 3-3.

The active Army's combat divisions also are changing. There will continue to be ten main combat divisions, but rather than have three brigades per division, plus three independent brigades (for a total of thirty-three combat brigades in the active force), the Army will add at least one brigade per existing division, for a total of forty-three, with the possibility of a further increase to forty-eight in 2007 or thereafter. Each unit will be somewhat smaller but more able to be independently deployed and operated than today's brigades. Of the forty-three planned brigades, twenty are envisioned as heavy forces, nine as light forces, five as medium-weight or Stryker brigades, and nine as airborne forces. Meanwhile, the Army National Guard's combat structure will change from its current composition—which includes fifteen enhanced separate brigades, nineteen brigades within divisions, and one (nonenhanced) separate brigade—to thirty-two brigade combat teams and one Stryker brigade combat team. In other words, the divisional structure will be eliminated but the overall number of brigades will not increase, in contrast with the number in the active Army.[27]

These smaller, more deployable brigade combat teams may make sense given improvements in Army firepower and the frequent demands of various small operations. However, it is worth noting that other plans have also been offered and may be just as good, including Colonel Douglas Macgregor's idea of eliminating the division and building larger brigades and battalions.[28] Regardless, medium-term restructuring of this type does not completely solve the current problem, which is that the Army is trying to do too much with too few people, particularly in Iraq.

Calculating the Need for More Troops

Despite all the laudable and promising initiatives mentioned, U.S. ground forces need an immediate increase in active duty troop levels. Personnel could be added to just the Army or to the Army and Marines in roughly proportionate numbers; regardless, they should be added to the active duty forces and added soon.

In fact, the decision is badly overdue. At the latest, it should have been made as soon as it became obvious in mid-2003 that the Iraq stabilization mission would be difficult and long. At first the administration assumed, imprudently, that it would be otherwise. According to Thomas White, former secretary of the Army, initial plans envisioned bringing 50,000 troops home within three months of the fall of Saddam and most of the rest three months thereafter.[29] Once those assumptions were shown to be wrong, policy should have been adjusted.

Given the limited benefits of all the steps mentioned above, even taken together, the Army should add more volunteer troops to its active duty forces, in addition to the 25,000 or so already added.[30] (Shortening deployments, an option recently considered by the Army, would not likely do much to ease the strain on soldiers since shorter deployments necessarily mean more frequent deployments for ground forces of a given size conducting missions of given strength.)[31] Ideally, to facilitate planning and reflect a strong national consensus behind the move, the increase in troop strength should be done through law by an act of Congress signed by the president. The Bush administration has resisted such a policy on the grounds that any such troop increase would be difficult to reverse in the future. But troop strength has been legislatively adjusted throughout modern American history and can be adjusted again when appropriate.[32]

Not only logic but a basic sense of fairness suggests that the United States should not generally send active duty troops back to Iraq after only a short respite at home. Spending one year in Iraq and one year (at most) at home and then going back to Iraq for a year is extremely demanding—

yet that is exactly what the Army will soon need to do with some units. For example, the 3rd Infantry Division, instrumental in overthrowing Saddam in 2003, has returned to Iraq.[33] Such a pace effectively turns soldiers into visitors in their own country, since the short time spent at home is dominated by the period of recovery from the previous deployment and then by preparation for the next deployment. The pace is also frantic for the Marines, who are opting for shorter deployments. In fact, some Marines of the 1st Division have already been to Iraq twice, with the real possibility of returning again by mid-2005.[34] Units such as the Army's 101st Airborne and 4th Infantry divisions are also likely to return to Iraq in 2005.

And, as argued convincingly by Lieutenant General James Helmly, chief of the Army Reserve, reservists should not have to be involuntarily activated for more than a nine-to-twelve month period once every five to six years. Given the expectations that individuals have when joining the National Guard or Army Reserve, any faster rate seems inconsistent with the notion of the part-time soldier and risky to the health of the reserves.[35]

How are planners to determine the most appropriate increase in the size of the Army? There is no definitive answer to that question. It is impossible to determine exactly how large the nation's rotation base must be to continue the Iraq mission over a period of years without causing undue strain on the all-volunteer force. The answer to that question will be known with certainty only after large numbers of people have been driven out of the military, at which point it will be clear that the force was indeed too small. But at that point, it could also be too late to fix the problem, since it will have become very hard to *increase* recruiting and retention levels and build up a larger force.

One simplified but still illuminating way to think about determining the necessary increase in troop strength is to imagine creating enough new units to conduct all deployments in the year 2006 or 2007. Army and Marine reservists also are being worked too hard, and therefore it would be desirable to create enough new capability to spell them as much as possible for at least a year.[36] In practice, of course, the United States would never depend entirely on fresh recruits for such demanding missions. But this simplification still conveys a proper sense of the scale of what is needed. Basically, most parts of the U.S. ground forces need to be given at least one more year at home than they are otherwise likely to have in the coming three to four years. The history of recent stabilization missions suggests that under some scenarios the number of troops in Iraq might decline to about 100,000 in the course of 2005–06, drop gradually to 50,000 or so in 2007–08, and perhaps remain at half the latter number for a period thereafter.[37]

So in rough terms, the United States might need 100,000 fresh troops for global missions in 2006–2007. Those numbers assume a brigade in Korea, one or two in Afghanistan, and about half a dozen in Iraq. Of that total, about 15,000 should be generated from existing and appropriate Pentagon plans to privatize certain current military positions or by introducing new efficiencies in areas such as the service secretariats and joint staff.[38] And 30,000 or more active duty troops might be available following the rebalancing of the forces discussed above, through which individuals in high-demand units are to be increased in number while units such as artillery are reduced in number. According to these calculations, some 40,000 to 50,000 additional troops still will be needed.[39] An increase in the overall size of the Army and the Marine Corps should provide it.

There are other reasons to think such an expansion possible, if it is done before a major crisis in recruiting develops. Even with such growth, the military would remain rather small—less than 1.5 million active duty personnel, in contrast to more than 2 million (out of a substantially smaller population base) during the later decades of the cold war. A 40,000 troop increase would amount to an increase of just 3 percent. Second, proper use of standard recruiting tools and incentives—advertisements, signing bonuses, and so on—can achieve much of the needed increase within two to three years. Finally, even if that proves not to be the case, changes to basic personnel policy that could bring more people into the military could (and should) be considered. More individuals could be brought into the military later in life, perhaps at somewhat higher levels than new recruits, if their technical skills warrant it. "Up or out" rules— which drive many good people out of the military once they reach a certain rank and fail to make the next promotion—can be relaxed. Retirement plans could be devised to provide government contributions to the accounts of individuals who do not wish to serve for twenty years and therefore do not qualify for the standard military retirement program. As Charles Moskos has advocated, some types of jobs could be filled by individuals on shorter tours of duty than the standard three to four years. Finally, for reservists, incentives like fuller compensation for lost pay could help attract and retain individuals who know their chances of being mobilized are now rather high.[40]

According to the Congressional Budget Office (CBO), it would take five years to recruit and fully train an additional 80,000 troops. That would be enough for two divisions plus associated support units, at an annual cost of about $6.5 billion just to maintain the forces stateside—not counting equipment investment costs, estimated at just shy of $20 billion.[41] CBO's methodology is too cautious, however, and its time estimate too pessimistic. Moreover, only about half that number of additional forces are needed; that means that a meaningful increase in the force can yield major benefits within a year of initiation.

Conclusion

The Bush administration has resisted any substantial or legislated expansion of the U.S. ground forces, even as it has used Army and Marine Corps forces at a torrid rate around the world. While its position is understandable—active duty forces are expensive and additional soldiers probably will be needed only for a few years—it is not convincing in the end. It risks breaking the all-volunteer force. That is, it risks making military service so unappealing that many in the military will start to leave when their tour of duty ends and the number of recruits will start to dwindle. Once such a process begins, it can become a vicious spiral, since the only antidote to losing people from the armed forces while war continues is to recruit even more, and that may not be possible, even if signing bonuses and pay are further increased.

No more time should be lost—at least 40,000 troops, mostly soldiers but perhaps some Marines as well, should be added to the U.S. military. At worst, this will prove to be unneeded insurance against the possibility of a major crisis in recruiting and retention. Just as likely, for the relatively modest cost of some $5 billion to $8 billion a year, it will help protect the current excellent all-volunteer military from experiencing a major personnel crisis—which could, if things got bad enough, necessitate a return to the draft, with its even greater problems, discussed in chapter 4.[42]

FOUR   # The Draft, the Overseas Base Structure, and the Allies

The question of whether U.S. ground forces should be increased in size is only one of several key issues concerning how the American military is structured and deployed abroad today. This chapter considers several other, related subjects, including whether the country needs specialized units for peacekeeping and other stabilization missions, whether it should restore the draft, how and where U.S. forces should be stationed abroad, and what help the American public can expect from its overseas allies. All of these issues are important in their own right, and in general the Rumsfeld Pentagon is making bold, smart decisions about how to address them. But as this chapter argues, even good policies in these areas are unlikely to change the conclusion that the United States needs more ground forces now and into the foreseeable future. Nor, with the possible and partial exception of greater burden sharing by U.S. allies, are these new policies likely to realize substantial cost savings.

Should the U.S. Military Build Dedicated Stabilization Units?

As the United States military has increasingly taken on constabulary duties—from Somalia in 1992–94 to Haiti, Bosnia, and Kosovo and to Afghanistan and Iraq today—some have argued that the country should create military or quasi-military units devoted especially to that task.[1]

The model for such a force might be the Italian *carabinieri,* a force of just over 100,000 that normally is under the control of the Ministry of Interior for police functions but that also can be used by the Ministry of Defense.

There is an obvious appeal to such an idea, given how frequently the United States has been deploying troops to support peace operations and stabilization missions. Regular combat troops do not always relish such tasks and are not fully trained for them. Specialized units could also be properly structured to include appropriate contingents of military police and of civil affairs and psychological operations experts.

There also are downsides to the idea, however—the most important being that in many peace operations it is necessary to deter renewed conflict. Or it may be necessary—as in Iraq, not to mention Somalia and Afghanistan—to prevail in a counterinsurgency campaign. Combat units, which are trained to win battles and inspire respect and fear in those who would challenge them, are best at those jobs.[2] Moreover, the military benefits from peace operations. Many of the commanders in Iraq who have been instrumental in the U.S.-led stabilization mission there "cut their teeth" on such activities in the Balkans and elsewhere—yet they also needed to be proficient in combat operations, since they were (almost unavoidably) the same people who led the invasion to overthrow Saddam.[3] Finally, in large operations, most notably in Iraq but also Bosnia in the early years, the missions are too large in scale (and, typically, too long in duration) for a small number of specialized units to handle on their own. Even if such units existed, they would require considerable help from general purpose formations.

For example, in Iraq, where some twenty-four active U.S. Army brigades and five National Guard brigades served in 2003 or 2004, no addition of one, two, or even three or four constabulary divisions to the force structure would have sufficed to handle the challenge. With a limited number of units available, would it have made the most sense to deploy them in places such as Basra or Mosul, where the counterinsurgency mission was the least demanding? Or would it have been best to deploy them to the Sunni triangle and Baghdad, where they would have been most needed given the difficulty of the job—but perhaps least well prepared for the rigors of combat? Alternatively, one could imagine using constabulary units for policing countrywide, overlaying them with smaller combat formations to fight the insurgency. But this distinction between policing and fighting is largely artificial in the context of a guerrilla struggle, so the logic for such an idea would be difficult to sustain; moreover, having two units share responsibility in any sector would complicate command arrangements enormously.[4]

Besides, the experience of recent stabilization missions suggests that often it is not combat units per se that are most lacking in capability. Their performance in maintaining the peace has generally been acceptable, and where missions have proven difficult it has been due to combat challenges (Lebanon, Somalia, Afghanistan) at least as much as peacekeeping challenges. Rather, the problem has most commonly been lack of proper planning for the stabilization missions, as well as lack of quickly deployable police officers, judges, criminal law experts, and other specialists in civil affairs who are needed yet generally unavailable.[5] In other words, U.S. troops are performing ably at policing, but planning and instruments for nation building are weak.

Given these considerations, the best course of action seems to be as follows. First, as the Army is already doing, the United States should add substantial quantities of the types of support units, like military police, that are frequently used in stabilization missions yet are in short supply. (Those with access to relevant highly classified information tend to argue that more personnel are needed within the human intelligence ranks of the intelligence community as well. It is difficult to assess that argument or to determine how many people are needed without more information, but an increase in funding of at least several hundred million dollars a year—corresponding to at least thousands of added linguists and other experts—seems appropriate.)[6]

Second, the United States should create nonmilitary units in other parts of the government that would be useful in any stabilization mission, as recently recommended by the Defense Science Board. Their specialties should include not only security activities but reconstruction assistance as well. The idea should not be to create capacity that already exists in the armed forces, nor should it be to pay for large standing formations of many thousands of police and aid officials. It would be inordinately expensive to maintain personnel permanently on standby in the United States for operations in countries the size of Iraq or Afghanistan, where standard sizing rules would suggest, for example, the need for up to 100,000 police officers during demanding stabilization efforts.[7] Rather, the smarter approach would be to put a nucleus of experts in various fields on the full-time government payroll; that group could become the core of any larger operation, drawing on standby reservists and nongovernmental organizations and private contractors to beef up their ranks as needed.[8]

Third, the Department of Defense should explore the creation of small teams designed to help plan and coordinate stabilization missions, and it should carry out realistic exercises using these planning groups as well as relevant parts of the force structure. In general, however, it should plan to use its normal forces for these types of tasks. At most, it might convert up to one active division and one reserve division to the stabilization mission, as recommended by Hans Binnendijk, Stuart Johnson, and Richard Kugler of the National Defense University.

Should the Draft Be Reinstated?

As casualties have continued to mount in Iraq, active duty forces have been heavily deployed, and frequent call-ups of troops from the National Guard and Army Reserve have placed unusual strains on many of the nation's citizen soldiers. Because of that, some have called for a return to military conscription. Congressman Charles Rangel of New York and former senator Fritz Hollings of South Carolina even introduced a bill in Congress that would restore the draft,[9] and one of Congress's most respected military veterans, Senator Chuck Hagel of Nebraska, has called for a serious national debate about the idea.[10] There has certainly been no serious planning for the possibility of a draft within the Rumsfeld Department of Defense, despite some allegations to the contrary by some organizations during the 2004 presidential race.[11] The question nonetheless remains: does it make sense? The short answer is no, given the outstanding quality of the all-volunteer force, which would surely be compromised by any plan to restore military conscription. But a fuller discussion of the pros and cons is appropriate.

It is important to note that in the war on terror the United States is indeed making far greater demands on some individuals than on others.

On one level, of course, that has always been true. Those who wind up being killed in war and the families that are left behind make the ultimate sacrifice, while those who are physically and psychologically wounded in combat and those who care for them also suffer enormous loss. But current policies amplify the inherent vagaries of military service. In particular, the fact that the military is an all-volunteer force, combined with the fact that certain regions of the country and certain parts of society contribute more than their share to that force, raises specific concerns. Some now assert, among other arguments, that policy elites, who are less likely than before to have served in the armed forces themselves or to have children who are presently serving, have become less sensitive to the possible human costs of the use of force.

There are indeed reasons to worry. It is not desirable for the country to have an increasing share of total military personnel come from only certain geographic regions, ethnic groups, or economic sectors of society.[12] On the whole, a much smaller percentage of today's population shows any interest in ever considering military service,[13] and, of course, far fewer lawmakers have military experience today than during the cold war.[14] In some ways, however, the fact that only a modest fraction of the population wishes to serve is just as well. Even as population has continued to expand, the modern American military is smaller than it has been in decades, and it cannot make room for everyone. But having large swaths of the country's population effectively opt out of military service cannot be good for the nation's cohesion. It is also troublesome that, even in the aftermath of the September 11 attacks, most Americans have made little or no financial sacrifice to support the government's antiterrorism efforts—they have even had their taxes cut in the face of large war supplemental appropriations and mounting deficits.

That said, the draft is not the answer. For one thing, the fact that certain groups serve disproportionately in the military means that the military offers opportunities to people who need them. Society asks a great deal of its military personnel, especially in the context of an ongoing war in Afghanistan and another in Iraq. But it also compensates them better than ever before—with pay, health care, educational opportunities, retirement pay, and the chance to learn skills within the armed forces that are often highly marketable thereafter. These various forms of compensation are quite high by historical standards, and they have eliminated any hint of a military-civilian pay gap except in certain relatively rare cases. Indeed, today's enlisted military personnel are now generally compensated considerably more generously than individuals of similar age and experience and educational background working in the private sector, once health and retirement benefits are factored in.[15] The military, while not without problems of discrimination and prejudice, is now among the most progressive institutions in America, providing many excellent opportunities for minorities and the economically disadvantaged.[16]

A few facts and figures back up these assertions—and also underscore the fact that today's military, while it includes more members of some groups than of others, is not dramatically unbalanced, racially or regionally. Enlisted personnel in the current American military are about 62 percent white, 22 percent African American (reflecting a fairly steady level since the early 1980s), 10 percent Hispanic, and 6 percent from other groups. In addition, minorities do not make up a disproportionate share of the personnel in the most dangerous jobs. For example, of the Army's 45,600 enlisted infantry in early 2003, only 10.6 percent were black, slightly less than the percentage of blacks in the general population.[17]

Moreover, one must be careful not to break an institution in the process of purportedly fixing it. The U.S. military is probably the most impressive in history—not only in terms of technology, but also in the quality of its personnel, their basic soldiering abilities, and their other skills, in fields ranging from piloting to computing to equipment maintenance to engineering to linguistics to civil affairs. Those who doubt this assertion need only review the decisiveness of recent American military victories in a range of combat scenarios, as well as the professionalism of U.S. forces in postconflict environments.[18]

With no disrespect intended to those who served in earlier generations, today's U.S. military is far superior to the conscripted forces of the past. Today's soldier, Marine, airman, airwoman, or sailor typically has a high school degree and some college, several years of experience in the military, and a sincere commitment to the profession that he or she has chosen. Contrast that with the ten- to twenty-four-month tours of duty that are inevitable in most draft systems; the small fraction of time that system leaves for a trained soldier to be in an operational, deployable unit; and the resulting mediocre quality of militaries that are still dependent on the draft (as in a number of European countries).

It is important to maintain a link between a society and its military. But that link is not so tenuous today as some assert, given the important role of the National Guard and Army Reserve in any overseas mission.[19] Even after completion of the ongoing reconfiguration of the Guard and Reserve and active duty forces, especially within the U.S. Army, their role will remain important in any future operation of significant scale and duration.

Moreover, the frequently heard assertion that policymakers have become insensitive to casualties is exaggerated. It was only a half-decade ago that the nation was purported to have the opposite problem, an extreme oversensitivity to casualties that prevented the country from considering decisive military actions that its national security required—and helping create a perception of American weakness that allegedly emboldened some adversaries.[20]

Someday, this assessment could change. The most likely cause would be an overuse of the all-volunteer force, particularly in the Army and Marine Corps, that led to an exodus of volunteers and a general perception among would-be recruits that service had become far less appealing. Clearly, a sustained period of high casualties in Iraq or another region would reinforce any such problem. At that point, to maintain a viable military, the nation might have no option but to consider the draft—though in an era of high technology and highly skilled armed forces, such a policy would surely create as many problems as it solved.

This conclusion does not categorically preclude the possibility of mandatory national service of some kind, with the military being one option from which individuals could choose. But only certain types of military jobs should be filled by those performing mandatory (and presumably rather short-term) service. The most demanding military positions should be reserved for professionals, as is the case today.[21]

Should the Reserve Component Have a Greater Role in Homeland Security?

Since 9/11, a number of analysts and politicians have advocated giving the Army and Air Force National Guard and the reserve components of all four branches of the military service a greater role in homeland security. Some say explicitly that they should therefore have a lesser role in military operations abroad; others merely imply the same conclusion in their main argument. Does the idea make sense?

The weight of evidence would seem to say no. Having the reserve component of the U.S. military involved in overseas combat missions is central to the post-Vietnam notion that the country should go to war only when its citizenry is broadly involved in the decision and in the conflict itself. Because the active duty military is much smaller as a percentage of the total national population than in past decades, and because it is concentrated in certain localities, this goal is best accomplished by continuing to use the National Guard and reserve units of the American military. Moreover, changing this approach would be extremely expensive, since reserve forces on average cost about half as much as active duty units of comparable size and capability, and—the most relevant issue for this discussion—reserve ground forces cost somewhat less than that.[22]

Still, it is true that the reserve component already is important in homeland security and that it should continue to be in the future, with its role perhaps even growing modestly for very specific purposes. Some reservists already help significantly, and they have done more in recent years. For example, there are a number of nuclear, biological, and chemical response teams in the reserve component. In addition, of course, National Guard infantry and police units as well as other forces would surely be employed if a major disaster required imposition of martial law or other drastic measures. There may be certain other specific roles that modest fractions of the reserve component could perform as well.

However, reservists are not well positioned to become the nation's primary line of defense against threats to the homeland. Most would arrive too slowly at any location where an attack had occurred to be as useful as firefighters, police, and health workers. Whether an attack involved chemical or biological agents, a radiological weapon, a collapsed building, or even a nuclear detonation, most victims of serious injuries would have to be treated before most reservists could be activated. And most security for the site in question would have to be provided by police, who could be on the scene quickly, rather than forces such as reserve infantry units, which might typically require twelve to twenty-four hours to mobilize. It is important to have a certain number of such infantry units and related forces dispersed around the country and available should a catastrophe occur. But their tasks would likely consist of maintaining public order over the longer term and perhaps ultimately cleaning up chemical or biological agents—not preventing terrorism or carrying out immediate consequence management. Thus they would not require training or equipment—or mission assignments—significantly different from those they currently have.

Nonetheless, this issue raises another. The reserve component may need to recruit more new members in the coming years—not to increase its size, but to ensure that the reserves do not include too many firefighters, police officers, and other first responders from any given community. Otherwise there is the risk that, should another terrorist attack (or even a natural disaster) occur in the United States while many reservists are deployed abroad, there may be too few first responders in a community to be effective.

What is the proper ceiling on how many first responders might be reservists in any given locality? It is difficult to be precise; localities probably need to be consulted for their input on this issue. They will often be pulled in two directions when making estimates. Planners would presumably prefer not to have many of their first responders taken away, but personnel chiefs would probably want to allow individuals that they know and value to perform military service (and make extra money) if that is what the individuals wish. Presumably by the time any group of first responders starts to have a double-digit percentage of its total strength in the military reserves, it could be handicapped by a large-scale military operation abroad.

The Army reserve structure is presently developing plans to address this problem. It hopes to find a way to ensure that no state ever has more than half of its reserve forces—and generally much less than that—deployed away from home at a time. Other aspects to such restructuring could involve smoother and faster mechanisms for sharing assets among states. This type of rethinking should make it feasible to use reserve forces for overseas missions without compromising their ability to respond to plausible demands at home.[23]

Can Overseas Base Realignment Ease the Strain on U.S. Forces?

In August 2004 President Bush announced the major contours of a new plan that has been under development since he became president to revamp how the United States stations its military forces overseas. The plan will dramatically reduce forces in Germany while shifting some troops to smaller facilities in eastern Europe, and it will scale back U.S. personnel in South Korea while repositioning many of those that remain in Korea. It might also add some facilities in Africa, where al Qaeda and its affiliates have been active.[24]

Fifteen years after the end of the cold war and three years into the war on terror, the plan generally makes good sense.[25] And despite the claims of critics and the anxieties of U.S. allies, it has been brewing for too long to be viewed as a reprisal against countries that challenged the Bush administration over the Iraq war, North Korea policy, or any other matter. Its rationale is clearly strategic, not vindictive. But it also has flaws that need to be corrected before it is put into place.

Prior to September 11, 2001, the United States had about a quarter-million troops abroad at any given time. Just over 100,000 were in Europe. Most of these were in Germany, which had 75,000 troops total, almost 60,000 of them soldiers. Another 13,000 were in Italy, almost 12,000 were in the United Kingdom, and smaller numbers were scattered elsewhere. Nearly 100,000 American military personnel were in East Asia, divided among Japan, South Korea, and the waters of the Western Pacific. About 25,000 were ashore and afloat in the Persian Gulf, and smaller numbers were found in Latin America and Africa.

Since 2001, U.S. capabilities in Europe and Asia have changed little, while now some 25,000 troops are in or near Afghanistan and more than 150,000 are in and around Iraq. Meanwhile the United States has withdrawn virtually all combat forces in Saudi Arabia and Turkey.

The Bush administration now wants to make other big changes too. Under the new plan, up to 70,000 troops will come home.[26] About 15,000 of them are currrently in Asia. The reductions will occur largely through consolidating redundant headquarters in Korea and Japan and taking one of two Army brigades permanently out of Korea. In Europe, at least half of the U.S. forces in Germany could either be brought back stateside or deployed in smaller numbers on shorter assignments to new bases in eastern Europe. The remaining Army forces in Europe would become lighter, with both heavy divisions now there likely to come home and at least one of the Army's new medium-weight Stryker brigades to replace them.[27] Some tactical combat aircraft could be shifted within the NATO region as well.[28]

Most of the Bush administration plan makes sense, at least on military grounds. In East Asia, the United States has complex and overlapping command structures in Hawaii, Japan, and Korea. Efforts to streamline them, while also moving U.S. military headquarters in Korea out of heavily populated Seoul, are long overdue.[29] Similarly, given South Korea's increasingly capable military forces, the U.S. Army's 2nd Infantry Division is no longer needed near the DMZ to help repel any initial North Korean onslaught. Better to deploy it south of Seoul, where it could prepare for an American–South Korean counteroffensive beyond the range of North Korean artillery. And one brigade is now probably enough; reinforcements would be needed in the event of war regardless.

Some criticize the decision to redeploy combat forces in the midst of ongoing negotiations with North Korea and advocate trying to obtain North Korean concessions in exchange for any such U.S. reductions and redeployments. Indeed, that would have been my preferred approach, as part of a negotiation strategy seeking a "grand bargain" with the Democratic People's Republic of Korea (DPRK) that attempted to push the Stalinist state toward major reforms as well as denuclearization.[30] But the reality is that the Bush administration is not likely to pursue such a strategy—and even if it did, at this point the negotiations could easily drag on for years. Meanwhile, the Army needs added forces for missions in Iraq and elsewhere now. In addition, should it become more committed to negotiations in the future, the United States would still have many other cards to play, notably in the economic and diplomatic realms, to elicit more favorable North Korean behavior. Indeed, a sufficiently able negotiator could portray the planned American reductions as a unilateral sign of good faith and absence of hostile intent, and perhaps ask Pyongyang for a reciprocal step now or in the future.[31]

As for Europe, rather than keep two of the U.S. Army's six heavy divisions in Germany, far from any plausible combat theater, there is a good argument that the Army should go for smaller, lighter, and quicker units.

As General James L. Jones, NATO's top commander, suggests, bases in Europe should be viewed as "lily pads" for regional and global deployments. Such a smaller, more mobile U.S. force in Europe would face fewer problems in training than it does now in heavily populated Germany. It could exercise more easily with new NATO members, and it would also provide a model of rapid deployability, which most European militaries need to emulate.

That said, there are still some problems with the administration's proposal for a new global strategic architecture. Consultations with allies—not to mention the Congress or the State Department—have been belated and insufficient, allowing misperceptions about the new basing plan to grow. As Joint Chiefs chairman General Richard Myers stated in testimony to Congress, "During . . . 2004 . . . Congress voiced concern over the Department's overseas basing plan. We are now in the process of detailed consultation with our allies and members of Congress."[32] That effort is quite belated. Unfortunately, the perception abroad that allies' views were not very important to the Bush administration in general and to the Rumsfeld Pentagon in particular may be hard to change now.

If taken too far, some of the changes proposed for the U.S. Army could worsen an overdeployment problem that is presently posing the greatest challenge to the all-volunteer force in its thirty-year history. Given the ongoing strain of the Iraq and Afghanistan missions, it simply does not make sense to take large numbers of Army soldiers out of bases in Germany, where they can be stationed with their families, and deploy them on unescorted tours to eastern Europe.

There is perhaps a marginal morale benefit to bringing forces home from Germany—though it is only marginal, since Germany is not a hardship post and soldiers there have their families with them.[33] Nonetheless, in today's military, soldiers may prefer staying stateside for longer periods of time so that their spouses can obtain work and so that their families can develop ties to one community—concerns that matter more for today's largely married force. The Army's plan to make it more likely that an individual will remain near one location for longer periods of time is a good idea consistent with the same logic.

For the foreseeable future, however, any new deployments abroad need to be very modest in scale. Nor should the budget implications of establishing new bases be overlooked—it is likely to cost a total of $5 billion to $7 billion in initial investment before realizing potential savings of $500 million to $1 billion a year thereafter.[34]

It is possible that the plan for relocating forces in Germany is too ambitious as well. Bringing home all four heavy brigades that are now there may be too much of a cut, reducing the opportunities for joint training and exercises with European heavy forces—a concern expressed by retired general Montgomery Meigs, former head of U.S. Army forces in Europe.[35] Leaving an existing heavy brigade there while introducing a Stryker brigade may make for a better mix and a more adequate overall set of capabilities. At a minimum, the possibility should be examined.

In contrast, the plan's likely effects on the U.S. Marine Corps do not go far enough. Notably, it does not appear to make major changes in the U.S. presence on Okinawa, where 20,000 Marines continue to be stationed on a densely populated island, implying mediocre training opportunities while causing local political problems and putting the broader U.S. base network in Japan at some risk.[36] The United States does need to store equipment on or near Okinawa and to have contingency access there in the event of a crisis, but it does not need to station most of the Marines now there on the island. Possibilities for relocating the Marines may involve other regional locations such as Korea, Australia, or Guam, but that is not yet clear.[37] This and other base relocation issues do need to be considered before the scheduled 2005 base realignment and closure (BRAC) process begins. Even though U.S. base capacity remains excessive and must be reduced to avoid wasting upward of $5 billion a year, it is important not to close bases that may later be needed, given the difficulty of obtaining the necessary land once the federal government has given it up.

Finally, a word of caution: maps can be deceiving. Bare-bones bases in landlocked central European countries may look as if they are close to likely combat theaters, but it can be harder to deploy equipment from such locations. European Command provided 54,000 troops for the Iraq mission from existing bases without long delays, profiting from Germany's excellent infrastructure and time-tested transportation procedures worked out between the United States and the German government.[38] Any new force alignment must be able to provide similar results in a similar time frame.

Table 4-1. *International Military Personnel in Iraq, October 2004*[a]

Country	Number of troops
Australia	920
Bulgaria	480
Italy	2,700
Japan	550
Netherlands	1,300
Poland	2,350
Romania	700
South Korea	2,800
Ukraine	1,450
United Kingdom	8,300
United States	138,000
Remaining nineteen coalition countries	2,150
Total	161,700

Source: Michael O'Hanlon and Adriana Lins de Albuquerque, "Iraq Index: Tracking Reconstruction and Security in Post-Saddam Iraq," updated October 25, 2004 (www.brookings.edu/iraqindex [October 25, 2004]).

a. In addition to the countries listed above, Albania, Azerbaijan, Czech Republic, Denmark, El Salvador, Estonia, Georgia, Hungary, Kazakhstan, Latvia, Lithuania, Macedonia, Moldova, Mongolia, Norway, Portugal, Singapore, Slovakia, and Tonga have troops in Iraq.

So some modifications of the Pentagon's plan, as well as much greater consultation with other parts of the U.S. government and other countries, are badly needed. But if Rumsfeld gets these things right, his new basing plan will merit strong support at home and abroad.

Can the Allies Do More?

Any analysis of U.S. troop needs must incorporate an assessment of what other countries can do and are likely to be able to do in the future. Carrying out peace operations, stabilization efforts, and humanitarian intervention missions is hardly just a U.S. responsibility.

That said, while many countries do provide modest numbers of forces for such missions (see tables 4-1, 4-2, 4-3, and 4-4), today few countries besides the United States are truly capable of projecting much military force quickly beyond national borders. Table 4-5 shows that about two-thirds of all such capacity resides in the U.S. armed forces—and an even higher percentage if one focuses on high-quality troops. Indeed, the United Kingdom, to some degree France and Australia, and to a lesser extent a

Table 4-2. *Military Personnel Participating in International Security Assistance Force (ISAF) Operations in Afghanistan, August 2004*[a]

NATO country	Number of troops	Non-NATO country	Number of troops
Belgium	250	Albania	81
Bulgaria	34	Austria	3
Canada	1,576	Azerbaijan	22
Croatia	22	Ireland	11
Czech Republic	19	New Zealand	84
Denmark	49	Sweden	19
Finland	47	Switzerland	4
France	565		
Germany	2,072		
Greece	127		
Hungary	130		
Italy	491		
Latvia	2		
Lithuania	6		
Luxembourg	9		
Netherlands	153		
Norway	147		
Poland	22		
Portugal	8		
Romania	32		
Slovakia	17		
Slovenia	18		
Spain	125		
Turkey	161		
United Kingdom	315		
United States	67		
Grand total	6,688		

Source: International Institute for Strategic Studies, *The Military Balance 2004/2005* (Oxford University Press, 2004), pp. 23–94.

a. Total does not include the separate U.S.-led Operation Enduring Freedom effort.

few other Western countries such as Italy possess the only other militaries capable of any significant rapid intervention missions whatsoever. This situation could change over time, offering some hope that demands on future American ground forces may be reduced as allied capabilities increase. But current plans for improvement are modest (see table 4-6). The added capability will probably be too slow in coming to help much

Table 4-3. *Military Personnel Participating in Stabilization Force (SFOR) Operations in Bosnia and Herzegovina, August 2004*[a]

NATO country	Number of troops	Non-NATO country	Number of troops
Belgium	4	Albania	70
Bulgaria	1	Austria	2
Canada	800	Ireland	50
Czech Republic	7	Latvia	1
Denmark	4	New Zealand	26
France	1,500	Sweden	7
Germany	1,000		
Greece	250		
Hungary	154		
Italy	979		
Lithuania	97		
Luxembourg	23		
Netherlands	1,000		
Norway	125		
Poland	287		
Portugal	330		
Romania	106		
Slovakia	29		
Slovenia	158		
Spain	935		
Turkey	1,200		
United Kingdom	1,100		
United States	839 (900)		
Grand total	11,084 (7,000)		

Source: International Institute for Strategic Studies, *The Military Balance 2004/2005* (Oxford University Press, 2004), pp. 23–94; Nicholas Wood, "Europeans Set to Succeed NATO in Bosnia," *New York Times*, December 2, 2004.

a. Numbers in parentheses represent the number of troops in Bosnia and Herzegovina in December 2004, where information is available.

with the current Iraq mission or even to significantly affect U.S. force planning in the foreseeable future.

Convincing allies to share more of the burden for interventions is not easy, even when the issues involved are less contentious than the current Iraq mission. Financial resources limit many countries' efforts—and it is difficult to convince another democracy to rethink its budget priorities to accord with a global security agenda that its citizens may not share or may prefer not to do their part to support.

Table 4-4. *Military Personnel Participating in Kosovo Force (KFOR) Operations, August 2004*

NATO country	Number of troops	Non-NATO country	Number of troops
Belgium	500	Argentina	113
Canada	800	Austria	535
Czech Republic	408	Ireland	104
Denmark	370	Sweden	650
Finland	820	Switzerland	220
France	2,900		
Georgia	140		
Germany	3,900		
Greece	1700		
Hungary	294		
Italy	2,530		
Lithuania	30		
Luxembourg	26		
Norway	60		
Poland	574		
Portugal	313		
Romania	226		
Slovakia	100		
Slovenia	2		
Spain	800		
Turkey	940		
Ukraine	325		
United Kingdom	1,400		
United States	2,060		
Grand total	22,840		

Source: International Institute for Strategic Studies, *The Military Balance 2004/2005* (Oxford University Press, 2004), pp. 23–94.

All that said, however, Western countries can do better. By emulating Britain and Australia, as well as the U.S. Marine Corps, they can acquire significantly more ability to deploy forces without increasing their budgets substantially. Reorienting defense priorities in order to buy enough dedicated strategic lift (ships as well as planes) and in-theater logistics support—such as mobile hospitals, equipment repair facilities, and old-fashioned trucks—can achieve a great deal. The fact of the matter is that, today, U.S. European allies are spending nearly half of what the United States does on their armed forces, yet they have no more than one-fifth as

Table 4-5. *Global Supply of Projectable Military Force, 2002*

Country	Total active ground strength (thousands)	Ground forces deployable in 1 to 3 months, sustainable for a year (thousands)	Percent of total quickly deployable
United States	649	400	62
United Kingdom	121	25	21
France	152	15	10
Germany	212	10	5
Italy	138	5	4
Canada	19	4	21
Netherlands	15	4	27
Denmark	13	1	8
Other NATO	949.2	20	2
European neutrals	95.4	5	1
Australia	24	5	21
New Zealand	4	0.75	19
Japan	149	5	3
South Korea	560	5	1
India	1,100	10	1
Pakistan	550	2	0.3
Bangladesh	120	0.3	0.3
Sri Lanka	95	1	1
Malaysia	80	2	3
Singapore	50	2	4
Russia	329	35	11
China	1,610	20	1
African neutrals	398.6	10	3
Argentina, Brazil, and Chile	300	12	4
Non-U.S. total	7,084.2	200 (approximate)	3 (approximate)

Source: Michael O'Hanlon, *Expanding Global Military Capacity for Humanitarian Intervention* (Brookings, 2003), pp. 56–57.

much overall deployable capacity. So there is a great deal of improvement possible even in the absence of defense budget increases, however desirable the latter might be in certain countries. Indeed, a prominent German think tank has recently made a similar argument, calling for Europe collectively to establish a goal of fielding 170,000 deployable forces.[39]

There are also a number of promising efforts to improve capacity outside the Western world. Several merit greater U.S. support. Perhaps the

Table 4-6. *NATO Deployable Force Structure*[a]

Country	Total deployable force	Number deployed abroad	Remaining deployable personnel
United Kingdom	25,000	15,000	10,000
France	15,000	10,000	5,000
Germany	10,000	7,000	3,000
Italy	5,000	9,000	0
Canada	4,000	3,000	1,000
Netherlands	4,000	2,500	1,500
Denmark	1,000	1,500	0
Other eleven countries in original nineteen	20,000	14,000	6,000
New members	1,000	200	800
Total	85,000	62,000 (approximate)	27,000 (approximate)

Sources: Michael O'Hanlon and Adriana Lins de Albuquerque, "Iraq Index: Tracking Reconstruction and Security in Post-Saddam Iraq" (www.brookings.edu/iraqindex [July 28, 2004]); Bastian Giegerich and William Wallace, "Not Such a Soft Power: The External Deployment of European Forces," *Survival* 46 (Summer 2004), pp. 163–82; Michael O'Hanlon, *Expanding Global Military Capacity for Humanitarian Intervention* (Brookings, 2003); NATO, "NATO in Afghanistan Factsheet," June 17, 2004 (www.nato.int/issues/afghanistan/factsheet.htm [January 6, 2005]).

a. The United States is not included. Most data are current as of summer 2004. Other prominent Western countries not listed here include EU members Austria, Finland, Sweden, and Switzerland as well as Australia, South Korea, and Japan. They add at least several thousand more potentially available troops. Australia in particular is not heavily deployed now, compared with past practices or capabilities; available data suggest that the Nordic countries and Austria also still have available forces.

The estimates of remaining deployable forces are generally conservative. Some countries may be able to deploy more forces than their theoretical maximum indicated above, if given sufficient preparation time and assistance with transportation and in-theater logistics support from other militaries, private firms, or on-site locals. Indeed, as noted above, Italy and Denmark already are doing so.

The following commitments for peacekeeping capability were made as part of the European Union "headline goals" at Helsinki in 2000: Austria, 2,000; Belgium, 1,000; Finland, 2,000; France, 12,000; Germany, 13,000; Greece, 3,500; Ireland, 1,000; Italy, 6,000; Luxembourg, 100; Netherlands, 5,000; Portugal, 1,000; Spain, 6,000; Sweden, 1,500; and United Kingdom, 12,500.

most striking is in Africa. After the 1994 Rwanda genocide, the Clinton administration launched a program in 1996 called the African Crisis Response Initiative (ACRI) to build Africa's capacity to respond to such crises. The goal was to train and equip seven to ten interoperable battalions, which, with airlift provided by others, could undertake complex humanitarian interventions effectively. More than 10,000 troops from Senegal, Uganda, Malawi, Mali, Ghana, Benin, Côte d'Ivoire, and Kenya have now been trained under this program and its successor, the African Contingency Operations and Training Assistance Program. Later, the Clinton administration also conducted Operation Focus Relief, a temporary but major program to prepare West African units for service in Sierra Leone. These steps marked a modest but important start based on the right vision. In the late 1990s, the UN also reviewed its peace operations capacity and afterward issued the Brahimi report, which stressed the urgent need for member states to make available to the UN rapidly deployable, trained, and equipped forces.[40]

During a February 2004 summit of the African Union, the European Union pledged $300 million toward the creation, training, and equipping of five regional, multinational standby brigades. The goal is that they should be able to handle traditional peacekeeping by 2005 and more complex peace enforcement or intervention missions by 2010. Principal credit must go to African nations themselves, which led in establishing the idea of the brigades, having learned from 1994 that certain human rights abuses are so extreme as to require external intervention in the internal affairs of sovereign states.

The idea of five rapidly deployable standby brigades, built of battalions from individual countries but each led by a multinational headquarters with adequate support elements, is precisely the right one. One such brigade, with 2,000 to 3,000 troops, could protect a threatened city or refugee camp or patrol a cease-fire line. Acting together, several of the brigades could even help to forcibly quell a mass killing like that in Rwanda a decade ago. Five brigades is not enough for the long term. But this initiative strikes a good balance, building a significant amount of capacity without overreaching. And according to recent reports, the Bush administration is now seriously considering providing substantial resources, on a scale of some $100 million a year, to similar efforts itself, though Congress resisted the idea throughout 2004.[41] Given the scope of the need and the acute humanitarian issues involved, Congress should support it.[42] At the G8 summit meeting in June 2004 at Sea Island, Georgia, the major industrial nations committed themselves further, to train and equip up to 75,000 troops capable of peace support operations by 2010, with a large fraction from Africa.[43]

The humanitarian imperative for action is sufficient reason to pursue this agenda. But the argument is not humanitarian alone, especially given al Qaeda's proven presence from Somalia to Kenya to West Africa.

Conclusion

In summary, increased burden sharing will not solve the Army's current problems. Even as the African Union brigades form and NATO develops its 20,000-strong rapid reaction force, global capacity for intervention will remain limited and improve only slowly.[44] Moreover, it is the Iraq mission, with its associated political radioactivity, that poses the most severe test to the U.S. military today—not some hypothetical future contingency in which greater burden sharing may or may not be a reality. More creative or careful diplomacy may be able to elicit greater allied support in Iraq, but that mission and others will place a greater strain on American military forces than they are able to prudently handle at their current size in the coming years.

Nor do other ideas discussed in this chapter alter the basic need for more ground forces or offer ways to substantially reduce the costs. A draft would be a poor idea, even if in theory it would allow the United States to reduce manpower costs by paying draftees less for their service. In this matter as with most others in life, you get what you pay for. The Bush administration's plan to bring home a substantial number of American military forces from Germany and South Korea has considerable arguments in its defense, but saving money is not really one of them. And adding dedicated units to the force structure for stabilization missions— probably not a good idea on military grounds in any case, unless done on a limited scale—would tend to increase rather than decrease overall costs, because it would not substantially reduce the need for combat forces.

A more promising avenue to finding defense budget savings, as discussed in chapter 5, is to scale back some of the military's ambitious weapons modernization plans. Even here, however, it should be underscored that realistically speaking, the goal is not to save money per se but to limit the magnitude of increases in expenditures in the future.

FIVE

Modernizing Weaponry

In the 1990s, the Department of Defense enjoyed a "procurement holiday," during which it bought less equipment than usual because it was downsizing the armed forces and because it could rely on stocks purchased during the Reagan era buildup. But like all holidays, this one had to end. The Bush administration is attempting to restore Pentagon procurement funding to a more historically typical share of the overall Department of Defense budget, usually about 25 percent. However, it has not yet achieved that goal, and cost pressures may prevent it from doing so in the future. Indeed, it is falling short of its own earlier targets for an appropriate level of procurement funding. That suggests a need for economizing wherever possible as the United States continues to modernize its military in future years. While it is important for weaponry to remain safe and serviceable and for modernization to occur in selected areas, the wholesale rush to replace most major weapons platforms with systems commonly costing twice as much is neither necessary nor affordable (see table 5-1).

It is possible to develop an alternative weapons modernization strategy by building on the great potential of modern electronics and computer capabilities. Such a strategy would not cancel every major weapons system: for example, F-22 and V-22 aircraft, advanced submarines, and next-generation littoral combat ships and the like would still have their place.

Table 5-1. *Selected Acquisition Report (SAR) Program Acquisition Cost Summary,*
June 2004[a]

Weapons system	Cost	Quantity
Army		
ATIRCM/CMWS	3,344.3	2,668
Black Hawk upgrade	15,093.0	1,221
Bradley upgrade	2,749.6	595
CH-47F	7,283.1	339
Excalibur	3,998.1	61,752
FBCB2	1,604.1	21,054
FCS	93,897.3	15
FMTV	18,464.1	83,185
GMLRS	12,420.4	40,239
HIMARS	4,706.3	894
Javelin	4,137.0	23,402
JTRS Cluster 1	20,809.7	109,002
Land Warrior	12,485.6	59,038
Longbow Apache	7,585.8	501
Longbow Hellfire	2,544.4	12,905
MCS	650.7	4,642
Patriot PAC-3	12,919.8	1,303
Stryker	8,779.9	2,096
WIN-T	12,625.1	1
Total	246,098	
Navy and Marines		
AESA (RDT&E only)	607.5	…
AGM-88E (AARGM)	1,551.6	1,790
AIM-9X	3,083.8	10,142
ASDS	1,984.1	6
CEC	4,488.8	279
Cobra Judy (RDT&E only)	1,495.1	1
CVN 21 (RDT&E only)	36,587.2	3
CVN–68	5,588.8	1
DDX (RDT&E only)	10,458.1	1
DDG 51	63,720.3	62
E-2C ADV Hawkeye	15,169.9	75
E-2C	4,364.8	44
EA-18G	8,610.3	90
EFV (AAAV)	10,750.7	1,025
F/A-18 E/F	44,459.0	462
H-1 upgrades	6,922.9	284

Table 5-1. *Selected Acquisition Report (SAR) Program Acquisition Cost Summary,*
June 2004[a] *(continued)*

Weapons system	Cost	Quantity
JSOW	4,484.8	12,334
LHD 1	10,069.1	8
LPD 17	15,800.9	12
MH-60R	10,707.1	254
MH-60S	6,055.5	237
MIDS-LVT	1,874.7	3,006
NESP	2,084.5	515
SM-2	906.4	160
SSGN (Trident conversion)	4,066.3	4
SSN 774 (Virginia Class)	84,380.2	30
T-45TS	6,411.5	210
T-AKE	4,555.3	11
Tactical Tomahawk	3,336.4	2,790
TRIDENT II MSL	37,841.3	568
V-22	48,697.0	458
Total	461,114	
Air Force		
AEHF	5,098.0	3
AMRAAM	10,912.0	10,999
B-1B CMUP	656.8	60
C-130 AMP	4,650.2	490
C-130J	16,626.1	168
C-17A	61,004.8	180
C-5 RERP	10,335.0	112
EELV	32,234.5	138
F/A-22	72,696.9	279
GBS	698.5	1,077
Global Hawk	6,368.8	51
JASSM	4,054.5	4,366
JDAM	5,375.7	209,752
JPATS	5,234.0	783
MINUTEMAN III GRP	2,502.7	652
MINUTEMAN III PRP	2,353.4	580
MP RTIP (RDT&E only)	1,587.5	...
NAS	1,422.5	92
NAVSTAR GPS	6,990.5	37
NPOESS	6,470.03	6
SBIRS High	10,125.4	5

Table 5-1. *Selected Acquisition Report (SAR) Program Acquisition Cost Summary,*
June 2004ª (continued)

Weapons system	Cost	Quantity
SDB	1,841.9	24,070
Wideband gapfiller	1,577.6	5
Total	270,817	
Department of Defense		
BMDS (RDT&E only)	67,046.0	...
Chemical demilitarization	24,704.1	32,196
JSF (F-35)	248,262.0	2,457
JTRS Waveform (RDT& E only)	996.1	...
Total	341,008.0	
Grand total	1,319,037	

Source: Department of Defense, "Selected Acquisition Reports (SAR) Summary Tables: June 30, 2004" (www.acq.osd.mil/ara/am/sar/2004-JUNE-SST.pdf [October 19, 2004]).

a. Millions of 2005 dollars. Totals may not add up due to rounding. Costs include past, current, and projected expenditures.

So would the Army's concept for the future combat system, further down the road, as well as missile defense. But in general, such extremely expensive next-generation weapons platforms would be purchased more selectively and in smaller numbers.

The Bush administration should not be blamed exclusively for its current weapons modernization agenda, which it largely inherited from its predecessors. Few new systems have been added to the procurement pipeline; it is virtually the same as the Clinton plan, with the exception of the Army's Crusader howitzer and Comanche helicopter and the Navy's lower-tier missile defense system, which have been canceled. That said, missile defense has received a major increase in funding, and allocations for some so-called transformational programs have been increased as well, as shown in table 5-2. Because of the latter programs, among others, the Pentagon's research, development, testing, and evaluation (RDT&E) budget has actually increased faster than the procurement account in recent years.

Part of the Bush administration's rationale for such large increases in RDT&E funds is its belief, shared by much of the U.S. defense community, that a revolution in military affairs is under way. The "revolution"

Table 5-2. *Highlights of the 2005 Acquisition Budget Request*[a]

System	Quantity	Cost (billions of dollars)
Army future combat systems	...	3.2
Army Stryker brigades	1 brigade (the 5th)	1.0
Marine Corps V-22	11	1.7
Navy carrier research	...	0.6
Virginia Class submarine	1	2.5
SSGN submarine conversion	...	1.2
DDG-51 destroyer	3	3.4
LHD-1 amphibious assault ship	...	0.2
LPD-17 amphibious ship	1	1.0
T-AKE cargo ships	2	0.8
DDX destroyer	1 (lead funding)	0.2
Littoral combat ship	1	0.1
Air Force F/A-22 Raptor	24	4.7
Joint strike fighter	...	4.6
Air Force C-17 transport	14	4.1
Navy F/A-18E/F	42	3.1
E-2C advanced Hawkeye control plane	...	0.6
EA-18G electronic warfare plane	...	0.4
Precision munitions	46,000	1.6
Joint unmanned combat air systems	...	0.7
Other unmanned aerial vehicles	Not specified	1.2
Transformational satellite communications	...	0.8
Joint tactical radio system	Not specified	0.6
Space-based radar	...	0.4
Cruise missile defense	...	0.2

Sources: Department of Defense, "FY 2005 Defense Budget," briefing slides, February 2004; and Steven M. Kosiak, "Classified Funding in the FY 2005 Defense Budget Request," *CSBA Update* (Washington: Center for Strategic and Budgetary Assessments, July 27, 2004).

a. Procurement plus research, development, testing, and evaluation. The last six systems, as well as the SSGN conversion, are deemed transformational programs by DoD (part of the SSGN conversion funding is listed under that category and part under the shipbuilding and conversion budget). The 2005 acquisition budget request of $143.8 billion ($74.9 billion for procurement and $68.9 billion for research, development, testing, and evaluation) includes $26 billion in classified funding ($12.9 billion in procurement and $13.1 billion in RDT&E).

thesis holds that further advances in precision munitions, real-time data dissemination, and other modern technologies, combined with appropriate war-fighting doctrine and organization, can transform warfare. The unprecedented rate of technological change, many observers hold, will sharply alter the size and composition of U.S. military forces—perhaps even saving money in the long run.[1]

That optimism needs to be tempered. Military technology is changing fast, but the rate of change may not outpace that of the past half-century. True believers in the "revolution" thesis invoke "Moore's law"—the tendency of the number of transistors on a semiconductor chip to double every eighteen to twenty-four months. They are right about the computer revolution, but they then often arbitrarily extrapolate from the trend in computer chips to predict equally rapid progress in entirely different realms of technology.[2] Such optimism is unwarranted.[3] Advances in electronics and computers do not necessarily imply comparably rapid changes in the basic functioning of tanks, ships, aircraft, rockets, explosives, and energy sources. Moreover, modernizing these latter types of major platforms is extremely expensive, so any hope that defense transformation will save money will be dashed unless the concept of transformation is defined carefully and as specifically as possible.

Indeed, too much fervor over a defense revolution or transformation can cause harm, leading to mistakes in fighting wars and also to misallocation of defense funds.[4] It has in the past: in World War I, when advocates of heavy artillery bombardment overestimated its benefits against enemy trench lines; in World War II, when advocates of strategic bombardment constantly promised benefits it did not always deliver; in the 1950s, when the creators of the U.S. Army's Pentomic divisions foolishly assumed that nuclear artillery could provide preparatory fire for infantry units; in Vietnam, where both the Army and Air Force relied too much on massive firepower.

In regard to the record of recent years, it is difficult to escape the conclusion that certain preparations for operations like those still going on in Iraq were not made because defense planners placed primary emphasis on high-technology transformational concepts. For example, inadequate investment was made in body armor, armor for vehicles, and flare countermeasures for helicopters.[5] Some such shortfalls persist even as of this writing, in late 2004.[6] Similarly, technologies such as nonlethal weapons, though advocated by some proponents of defense revolution, tended to receive limited funds even though there is a strong case for spending several times the recent average of $25 million a year on them.[7] When advocates of transformation place principal emphasis on expensive high-tech weapons platforms, they are particularly prone to skewing military investment priorities. This perspective should be kept in mind as individual weapons systems are evaluated.

Another problem with a platform-oriented approach to modernization is that the military services and the defense industry do not place enough emphasis on interoperability. Even today, weapons often are built in a way that does not permit easy integration with those used by other branches of the armed forces until expensive modifications are specifically requested by the Pentagon. As Admiral Edmund Giambastiani, the head of Joint Forces Command, has argued, that practice must change.[8]

In sum, the broad philosophy of U.S. defense modernization should encompass three main themes:

—Replace or refurbish all major equipment quickly enough to keep it safe and reliable.

—Purchase only a modest number of high-cost next-generation weapons platforms, such as F-22 fighter jets and advanced submarines, and otherwise make do with somewhat less advanced technology (such as F-15s and F-16s).

—Aggressively modernize electronics, sensors, precision munitions, unmanned vehicles, and related technologies that exploit the ongoing revolution in computing and miniaturization and offer maximum benefits for the cost. These capabilities often can be retrofitted on existing weapons platforms, effectively modernizing them without requiring expensive replacement.

Missile Defense and Space Systems

In 2005, the Bush administration increased funding for missile defense to about $10 billion a year (see table 5-3). That doubles the nearly $5 billion in funding it inherited in 2001—which was itself almost as high as missile defense funding under Ronald Reagan and George H. W. Bush and more than twice the amount budgeted before President Reagan's Strategic Defense Initiative speech in 1983 (see figure 5-1).[9]

Table 5-3. Missile Defense Budget, 2005 Budget Request[a]

System	2002	2003	2004	2005	2006	2007	2008	2009
Patriot system (PAC-3) procurement	751	767	829	585	N/A	N/A	N/A	N/A
Patriot system (PAC-3) RDT&E	132	141	159	65	N/A	N/A	N/A	N/A
Basic technology	119	139	228	207	202	249	290	309
Advanced concepts, evaluation, and systems (ACES)	—	—	152	260	233	235	235	228
Terminal phase defense	1,689	1,214	887	951	1,007	1,134	578	416
Midcourse phase defense	4,136	3,281	3,796	4,466	3,111	3,130	1,907	1,827
Boost phase defense	719	776	626	500	564	621	481	463
Sensors	520	404	431	600	801	1,474	1,138	1,250
Interceptors	...	...	120	518	1,135	1,741	2,228	2,483
Testing and targets	...	...	645	726	682	665	663	698
Products	...	...	309	425	427	452	463	477
Core activities	...	...	451	487	500	535	547	576
Other	117	872	593	158	161	160	167	171
Total	8,183	7,594	9,226	9,948	8,823	10,396	8,697	8,898

Source: Patriot PAC-3 procurement and RDT&E 2002: Department of Defense, "Program Acquisition Costs by Weapon System: Department of Defense Budget for Fiscal Year 2003," February 2002 (www.dod.mil/comptroller/defbudget/fy2003/fy2003_weabook.pdf [March 23, 2004]). Patriot PAC-3 procurement and RDT&E 2003–05: Department of Defense, "Program Acquisition Costs by Weapon System: Department of Defense Budget for Fiscal Year 2005," February 2004 (www.defenselink.mil/comptroller/defbudget/fy2005/fy2005_weabook.pdf [March 23, 2004]). All figures above for 2002: Missile Defense Agency, "FY 2002 Authorization Funding Track" (www.acq.osd.mil/bmdo/bmdolink/pdf/budget.pdf [March 22, 2004]). All figures above for 2003: "FY 2003 Authorization Funding Track" (www.acq.osd.mil/bmdo/bmdolink/pdf/fy03auft.pdf [March 22, 2004]). All figures above for 2004–09: Missile Defense Agency, "FY 2005 Budget Estimates," February 18, 2004, p. 21.

a. Millions of 2005 dollars. In 2004, PAC-3 procurement and RDT&E were moved from the Missile Defense Agency budget to the Army budget. The budget for the Missile Defense Agency was $8.07 billion (2002), $7.49 billion (2003), $7.6 billion (2004), and estimated at $. 9.2 billion (2005), $8.7 billion (2006), $10.3 billion (2007), $8.6 billion (2008), and $8.8 billion (2009). Revisions were made to the program element structure of ballistic missile defense funding in 2004. The Ballistic Missile Defense System program element was decomposed into three separate program elements: Core, Products, and Testing and targets. Two new program elements were added in 2004: Interceptor and Advanced concepts, evaluations, and systems (ACES).

Figure 5-1. *Historical Funding for the Missile Defense Agency and Its Predecessors*[a]

Billions of dollars

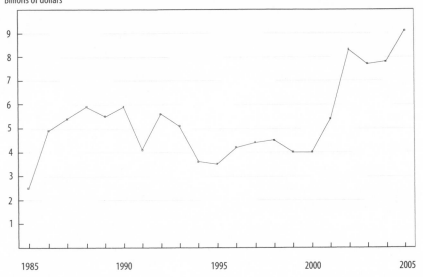

Source: Missile Defense Agency, "Historical Funding for MDA FY85–05" (www.acq.osd.mil/mda/mdalink/ pdf/histfunds.pdf [November 5, 2004]).

a. Historical funding levels are for the Strategic Defense Initiative Organization (SDIO), the Ballistic Missile Defense Organization (BMDO), and the Missile Defense Agency (MDA). SDIO was the predecessor to the MDA. In 2004, PAC-3 procurement and RDT&E was moved from the Missile Defense Agency budget to the Army budget. Army-related missile defense funding is not included in the graph.

Despite the demise of the U.S.-Russian Anti-Ballistic Missile Treaty and the absence of any proposals to restore it or develop something similar, strategic missile defense remains a hugely controversial subject. The controversy is due to the imperfect state of the technology involved as well as the high budget cost—and potential further diplomatic cost—of deploying it.

The Pentagon is deploying several interceptors that—although they were still experiencing problems in testing through 2004—should become capable of shooting down long-range warheads from a country such as North Korea. The first was installed in July 2004.[10] By the end of 2005, a total of twenty interceptors will be stationed on land, in Alaska and California, with ten more at sea. Radar to detect incoming missiles and track their warheads will be located on land and at sea and a number of existing sensors will be improved (as done with a half-dozen destroyers by equipping them with Aegis radar).[11] According to plans, more interceptors would be added over time at various sites in the United States and at sea, including a shorter-range land-based interceptor known as THAAD and quite possibly multiple-warhead defensive missiles to improve the original midcourse system, based in Alaska and California. Sea-based interceptors would be built, an airborne platform using a laser would add more defensive firepower, and at some point land-based interceptors designed to shoot down an enemy rocket in its boost phase could be developed as well and deployed overseas near possible launch points. Ultimately, depending on the evolution of the potential threat as well as allied views on the matter, an additional site might be built in eastern Europe.[12]

No space-based weapons would be included in the architecture, given current threats and available technologies.[13] But sensor networks would eventually be improved to include two new satellite constellations for detecting missile launches and tracking warheads. Eventually, space-based weapons platforms might be considered.[14]

As critics point out, the missile defense programs now being deployed are far from mature. In the Alaska–California system, a large, three-stage defensive rocket would ascend just above the atmosphere before releasing a small homing vehicle that would maneuver itself into the path of an incoming reentry vehicle that could carry a nuclear or biological weapon. The resulting high-speed collision would destroy the weapon. While "hit to kill" technology has shown some promise and produced some actual destructive intercepts on the test range, especially with a shorter-range system, a number of tests of the Alaska–California system have failed. And even those that have succeeded have involved surrogate components, like a slower defensive rocket, not the actual three-stage version intended for deployment. They also have needed help in finding and tracking the target warheads, since not all parts of the intended sensor network have yet been built.[15] As Lieutenant General Ron Kadish, then the director of the Pentagon's missile defense efforts, put it, "The idea of fly before buy is very difficult for this system. This is fly as we buy."[16]

But even if the technology is rushed, and even if the Bush deployment timelines were partly political, deploying an interim missile defense capability makes sense. Since the United States has had absolutely no missile defense capability, strategically speaking even an imperfect system is better than the status quo. This is not a question of replacing an existing proven weapon, like an F-15 fighter aircraft or transport helicopter, with a new technology like the F-22 or V-22. Rather, deploying basic missile defense quickly is more analogous to building rudimentary fortifications or throwing up barricades when a city is otherwise entirely open to invaders. Another good analogy might be the use of JSTARS radar reconnaissance aircraft in Operation Desert Storm. At the time, the United States had only two such aircraft, and they were developmental designs rather than proven systems. But because the Department of Defense had no other platform capable of surveying large swaths of territory to find moving objects in bad weather or at night, deploying JSTARS made sense, and it yielded appreciable benefits. Moreover, the long-range missile threat should not be ignored. North Korea surprised the U.S. intelligence community once, in 1998, with a partially successful test of a three-stage rocket. There is no way to be sure it could not do so again—or even field a workable missile—on short notice.

Some will argue that a country like North Korea will never strike the United States with a long-range missile, since doing so would ensure the regime's demise. That argument is right, under most circumstances. But Pyongyang might feel more emboldened to provoke a security crisis and attempt to extort resources from the United States and its neighbors if it had a long-range missile. And in the unthinkable event that war ever again occurred on the Korean Peninsula, it would be desirable to minimize the chances that a dying but nuclear-armed North Korean regime could take an American city down with it.

Since missile defense is not the country's top security priority, however, some perspective is in order. Even as it continues to deploy an interim long-range missile defense capability, improve shorter-range missile defense systems, and work on technologies for better future systems, the United States should scale back its missile defense plans. In broad terms, a level of spending between that of the late Clinton years (when funding was primarily for research and development) and the current Bush level would be appropriate. That would allow for deployment of perhaps a two-tier strategic defense system, featuring the Alaska–California midcourse system and one other type of defensive capability. Such an architecture could be designed to intercept a number of warheads—but not more than a few dozen. Further improvements in theater missile defenses and ongoing research and development of improved technologies for strategic defense would be possible as well, albeit at a more gradual pace. The strategic deployment would cost perhaps $40 billion, equaling $2 billion to $3 billion a year; missile defense overall would cost $7 billion to $8 billion a year.[17] (The administration's 2006 budget request is around $8.5 billion, a substantial cut, but future plans are unclear.)

A scaled-back version of the existing Bush missile defense program might include several economies—first among them reduction of the effort to provide missile defense systems originally designed to intercept slower and shorter-range missiles with long-range missile defense capability. Notably, the $1 billion in the 2005 budget proposal intended to help convert the Navy Aegis defense system into a strategic defense system could be scrapped. Upgrading some radar systems to help with early warning may make sense, but it is far from clear that the integrated Aegis system including interceptor missiles will work against high-speed intercontinental warheads.[18] Second, the scale of any deployment of the main midcourse system could be limited to fifty to 100 interceptors, enough to deal with the more plausible threat of a North Korean attack but not enough to handle a concerted Russian attack; their effectiveness would fall in a gray area vis-à-vis China. Third, overall program development might be slowed, given that plausible overseas threats have been delayed by North Korea's continued testing moratorium and the overthrow of Saddam Hussein.

Fourth, the multitude of missile defense programs could be scaled back somewhat in number. The Navy's lower-tier missile defense system was already eliminated, for mediocre performance. But it may be necessary, depending on the future progress of the technologies, to cancel another system too. Candidates could include the airborne laser (ABL), which is experiencing significant development problems, or (if ABL works well) a kinetic-energy boost-phase interceptor program.[19]

A fifth and final set of concerns relates to space-based assets. Certain technologies designed to enhance the performance of missile defense systems, but perhaps not worth the money—notably, the planned STSS constellation of low-orbit tracking satellites—might be canceled. Neither space-based missile defenses nor dedicated antisatellite (ASAT) programs are needed. Ground-based missile defense programs provide ample latent ASAT capability, and the United States benefits too much from the status quo in space—where it can target and communicate with virtual impunity but others cannot—to wish to change the situation anytime soon.[20]

Space programs should emphasize greater hardening of American military satellites against attack as well as improving ways to deal with jamming—especially for GPS systems, meaning that next-generation GPS satellites are needed.[21] In addition, satellite systems should improve the military's ability to know whether satellites have been attacked. The armed forces also should explore dedicated communications systems such as those using laser technology, given the importance of dependable communications systems and the potential vulnerabilities of current commercial carrier satellites.[22] They should not, however, be unrealistic—as seems to be the case, for example, with the space-based radar constellation concept, whose development Congress has rightly slowed given the expense and technological immaturity of the system.[23] Nor should they move toward dedicated antisatellite weapons programs, at least not now—though improved ways to jam adversarial satellites in a nondestructive fashion, which are now being fielded, are appropriate.[24]

The Air Force

The Air Force's equipment is generally still quite capable, especially by international standards, but it is aging rather fast. Fighter fleets were purchased mostly in the 1970s and 1980s; refueling and transport and combat support aircraft are typically at least as old. The dilemma for the Air Force is that its modernization programs are generally so expensive that it will be quite hard to replace the aging systems fast enough, unless a more economical procurement strategy is devised that allows more planes to be purchased for a given sum of money. Even under existing plans, by 2012 fighter aircraft will grow in average age from seventeen to twenty years, for example, and airlift and tanker fleets will remain quite long in the tooth (with average ages remaining at about twenty-four years and forty years respectively).[25] And those plans, given their expense, may slip, leading to even higher ages.

The two main Air Force combat weapons programs are the F/A-22 Raptor and joint strike fighter (JSF) programs. The first has entered production and is expected to turn out about 300 stealthy aircraft that originally were designed to ensure U.S. air supremacy but—after the end of the Soviet threat and the corresponding lessening of the need for a new state-of-the-art fighter—were also given the mission of ground attack. The second is a huge program developed to produce, in conjunction with the Navy and Marine Corps, some 2,500 less expensive but still modern stealthy ground-attack aircraft. The Air Force would purchase more than 1,700 of these planes, replacing its workhorse F-16 fleet with them over time.[26]

But the need for two large-scale aircraft modernization programs in such rapid succession is open to serious doubt. For one thing, American aircraft have conducted recent operations with stunningly few losses, raising questions about the need for whole fleets of stealthy airplanes. Notably, in roughly 20,000 sorties in Operation Iraqi Freedom in 2003, no aircraft were lost in air-to-air combat and only two fixed-wing aircraft (as well as five helicopters) were lost to Iraqi ground fire.[27]

Second, the performance of existing aircraft in attack missions has continued to improve markedly due to the introduction of improved electronics and sensors. Better targeting and communications systems that direct weapons to their proper aimpoints quickly and lethally have also enhanced combat capabilities. Third, refurbishing or replacing existing aircraft with similar kinds of planes (notably, F-16s) would be substantially less expensive than buying new stealthy aircraft. There also are clever ways to get more out of each existing plane, such as building smaller bombs so a greater number can be delivered per sortie and perhaps putting air-ground munitions on F-15C air superiority fighters.[28] Fourth, the increased performance of unmanned aerial vehicles raises doubts about the JSF in particular; planning to buy such huge numbers of manned airplanes throughout the next decade may be technologically backward. Unmanned combat aerial vehicles are technically feasible; in fact, their development is progressing well.[29] The greatest challenges now are learning "to fly and fight with them," in the words of a former senior Air Force technology expert—a challenge that should not take decades to solve.[30]

There is a strong argument that the F/A-22 Raptor is not needed and that refurbished or new F-15s would satisfy the country's security requirements adequately for years to come. But a case can be made for continuing with the program as scheduled given the mature state of the F/A-22 program as well as its new capabilities as an attack aircraft—and the potential rise of a new and more technologically advanced threat, such as from China. Reports of a recent set of mock dogfights in which Indian air force pilots flying Russian- and French-built aircraft frequently defeated visiting U.S. F-15s—admittedly with a greater number of planes on the Indian side—add further credence to the argument.[31] Since more than $40 billion has now been spent on the program and more than sixty airplanes authorized for purchase, it makes sense to get something out of the effort.[32]

That said, there is no compelling case for the currently planned number of fighters, and a smaller fleet of 150 or so would still provide as many air superiority fighters, which are designed to control airspace, as the U.S. Air Force has recently used in major regional wars. Cutting the F/A-22 program in half in this way and buying or refurbishing F-15Cs to replace the Raptors that would have been built would save about $50 million an airframe, or some $7 billion over the course of the program, averaging about $500 million a year. The refurbishing also could be done fairly quickly, reducing the risk that the nation's combat air fleet will suddenly develop serious problems and become difficult to keep operational. The administration's own plan as reflected in the 2006 budget request is similar (179 aircraft), but the Air Force and much of the Congress may oppose such cuts.

Even more important, the joint strike fighter program should be further revamped. The program has already been scaled back but remains much too big. As long as the main variants of the JSF continued to be developed, particularly the Marine and Air Force versions, it could be done in a way to protect roles for key foreign partners. The latter now include the United Kingdom, Italy, Turkey, Israel, the Netherlands, Denmark, Norway, Canada, and Singapore. First of all, it is a fairly rushed program that has experienced some technical difficulties (such as excessive weight in the short take-off and landing version).[33] In addition, F/A-18E/F Super Hornets (for the Navy) as well as the F/A-22 are still being produced. For these reasons, the JSF can be delayed by at least two to three years and perhaps as long as half a decade if major allied partners agree.

Second, over the longer term, instead of purchasing 2,500 joint strike fighters, the military should instead buy about 1,000. The Air Force could buy a few hundred short–take-off variants of the JSF (now being designed just for the Marine Corps) to hedge against future threats to its airfields, as Air Force officials themselves have recently advocated.[34] It could otherwise refurbish or buy upgraded versions of current planes, such as the new F-16 Block 60 aircraft, as quickly as necessary to keep its core combat forces flightworthy and safe. Over time, it could probably buy unmanned combat aerial vehicles as well. The net savings from these changes could approach $50 billion. Nearly half of those savings would occur over the next ten years, making for annual savings of about $2 billion.[35]

Another area of sensible saving within Air Force (and Navy) budgets is in the U.S. nuclear weapons arsenal. In May 2002, the United States and Russia agreed to reduce their number of operational strategic warheads to between 1,700 and 2,200 by 2012, roughly one-third of current levels. The Moscow Treaty does not require those reductions to happen quickly, nor does it require them to be made in any particular way. But given the reduced importance of large strategic arsenals in the world today—and in keeping with the spirit of the treaty—the United States could choose to cut its nuclear forces to the appropriate levels quickly and in a manner designed to save money.

Specifically, the United States could eliminate some Minuteman missiles and Trident submarines, exceeding its current plans to eliminate the country's arsenal of fifty MX missiles, convert four (of eighteen) Trident submarines to an all-conventional use, and conduct a similar conversion of the country's eighty-one B-1 bombers to an all-conventional use. The Congressional Budget Office estimates that retiring 200 Minuteman missiles and two more Trident submarines could save nearly $1 billion a year.

Indeed, the United States and Russia should aim for a follow-on to the Moscow Treaty, of similar simplicity and informality, that would reduce all nuclear warheads to a level of between 1,000 and 1,500. That would preserve the symbolic trappings of superpower status for the two countries—and obviate the undesirable and complicating measure of bringing other nuclear powers into the process—while further marginalizing nuclear weapons in U.S. and Russian security policies.[36] Enough warheads would remain for a robust deterrent with a wide range of capabilities against different targets. In this event, Department of Defense budgets could realize further savings of a magnitude comparable to that estimated above for possible savings under the Moscow Treaty.

Additional savings might be found by scaling back some activities of the Department of Energy's nuclear weapons establishment. The United States might even change its traditional three-laboratory philosophy somewhat, scaling back the role of either Los Alamos or Livermore in nuclear weapons stewardship and design.[37] The case for new, more advanced nuclear weapons designs, such as earth-penetrating warheads, is far too weak on technical and strategic grounds to justify either major new development programs or resumption of nuclear testing.[38] For example, such warheads could not penetrate the ground deeply enough to prevent the problem of nuclear fallout. Moreover, the case for building a large plutonium pit production facility is unconvincing. The existing capability at Los Alamos can be configured to produce more than fifty pits a year—consistent with an arsenal of at least 1,000 warheads and perhaps twice that, which is ample. The $4 billion investment required for a new pit facility is unneeded. On balance, these changes at the Department of Energy could save an average of at least $500 million a year.[39]

The Army

The Army has come closest to following the rhetorical exhortations of George W. Bush, who when campaigning at the Citadel in 1999 called on the U.S. military to "skip a generation" of weaponry and hasten development of more futuristic technologies. The Army has canceled its Crusader artillery system, deemed too heavy to be quickly transportable, as well as the Comanche reconnaissance and light-attack helicopter, which continued to encounter delays. The latter cancellation was initiated by the Army itself, which elected to put saved funds into improving the survivability of existing helicopters. It is thus not a harbinger of the end of the manned attack helicopter, despite the difficult experiences of the 11th Aviation Regiment near al-Hilla, Iraq, in March 2003. In that engagement, little damage was done to enemy forces while most of the thirty U.S. Apache helicopters involved were damaged to the point that they could not be flown and one was shot down. But the Apaches were thrown into a hastily prepared operation without other air or artillery support and with overly demanding rules of engagement that required positive identification of targets—which led in turn to having helicopters hover near enemy forces. More flexible and appropriate tactics would—and, in Iraq and elsewhere, generally did—produce better results.[40]

In regard to future acquisition policy, the most notable program is the future combat system (FCS). It is basically the Army's next-generation replacement of the main battle tank as well as other major elements of the current heavy divisions. It is designed to weigh much less than an Abrams tank, therefore to be more easily deployed and fuel efficient and also to depend more on information networking than on heavy armor to survive (in other words, it will depend for its survival largely on not being shot at). The goal is for it to fit on a C-130 aircraft, suggesting size and weight characteristics similar to the Stryker's (see below). The future combat system is actually a family of eighteen different types of systems, some to be manned and others unmanned—though it is difficult to learn much from Army literature about the specific attributes of any of the variants.[41]

Until recently, FCS production was planned for 2008, with initial operational capability by 2010 and one-third of the Army fielding FCSs by 2020. Now the plan is to delay somewhat, building an experimental unit by 2008 and brigade-sized operational capability by 2014.[42] Total cost of these efforts is estimated at $92 billion.[43]

This concept is understandable in many ways. Heavy divisions are slow to deploy, dependent on huge logistic footprints, and increasingly vulnerable. Also, they may be less needed today, given the capabilities of modern airpower as well as the demise of the Warsaw Pact and the Iraqi threat. Trying over time to make heavy divisions lighter and more deployable makes sense.

But the FCS plan goes too far too fast. For one thing, it discounts the utility of heavy tanks too quickly. For all their downsides, they have continued to perform impressively in modern war (see chapter 2), and they provide protection in settings, such as the streets of post-Saddam Iraq, that may continue to be of critical importance.[44] In addition, the modernization program is badly rushed. Technologically speaking, progress in armor and propulsion systems and other key components of modern military vehicles has been slower than the Army seems to assume.[45] Moreover, the program to build a half-dozen medium-weight Stryker brigades is relatively new. Indeed, it is ongoing. It makes sense to learn more about its strengths and weaknesses before committing to the next modernization effort. Once Stryker has been more thoroughly tested, in Iraq and elsewhere, and once the underlying technologies needed for the FCS have been more thoroughly investigated, the Army's next-generation weaponry and its associated "objective force" will be more appropriate than they are now.[46]

The earlier generation of Abrams tanks, Bradley fighting vehicles, and other platforms remains in generally reasonable shape; there is no need to rush to replace them. Slowing pursuit of the main objectives of the existing FCS program by as much as another half-decade therefore seems reasonable. That would space successive generations of major Army weaponry about fifteen years apart—still a rapid rate of modernization—and would save an average of $2 billion a year during the period of postponement, since the FY 2006 budget request is for more than $3 billion and additional increases appear to be slated for subsequent budgets.[47]

The Navy and Marine Corps

Besides the JSF and nuclear weapons programs discussed above, several other programs for the Navy and Marines merit scrutiny. They include the V-22 tilt-rotor aircraft, as well as the Virginia class submarine and DD(X) destroyer programs. These services also need some equipment fairly soon—or, more to the point, they need to develop sustainable and healthy procurement strategies because at present they are not buying weaponry in sufficient quantity to maintain their force structure over time. That is particularly true for the Navy.

The Marine Corps's V-22 tilt-rotor aircraft is a questionable idea. Its expected survivability in combat is estimated to be only about 10 to 20 percent better than that of a helicopter—and perhaps less than that, given restrictions that may have to be placed on its flight profile due to the aerodynamic dangers that have caused tragic accidents in recent years. Indeed, it is even possible that the V-22 will be less survivable than helicopters. There are means to avoid the aerodynamic issues that caused V-22 accidents in the past,[48] but according to Thomas Christie, the Pentagon's director of operational testing and evaluation, flight procedures designed to avoid the vortex ring state that led to earlier crashes may be difficult to follow correctly when facing hostile fire, increasing the risk that this dangerous condition could recur.[49] Before the vortex ring condition was even discovered, then-Secretary of Defense Dick Cheney tried to end the V-22 program (Congress and then the Clinton administration ultimately overruled him).

Even if the V-22 works, the Marines will still need helicopters to transport some of their heaviest equipment, meaning that the nature of amphibious assault operations will not change radically in any event.[50] Viewing the V-22 as a technology development program—and a means of buying modest numbers of aircraft for special operations and other niche missions demanding the V-22's speed and range—would be a sounder course of action. This approach would suggest a modest purchase of just a few dozen V-22 aircraft, plus ample numbers of existing helicopters—which, again, can be done as quickly as reliability and safety concerns dictate, a major advantage of a less ambitious and less costly modernization strategy. Accounting for the need to purchase new helicopters to provide the lift that the V-22 would have, net savings would total approximately $10 billion over the life of the program, or some $750 million a year.[51]

In regard to nonlethal weaponry, a recent Council on Foreign Relations task force has made a compelling suggestion to expand funding to $300 million a year. Such weapons, developed in the recent past under Marine Corps guidance, are important not only for peacekeeping but also for crowd control and self-defense in hostile environments in places such as Iraq. By reducing the number of innocent people hurt—and thus the number of individuals who take up arms to avenge the harm done, even if inadvertently, to friends and family—such weapons can help American forces improve their prospects for success.[52]

Before moving on to ships, a brief word is in order on the Navy's variant of the JSF. The Navy might even consider getting out of the JSF program entirely, to avoid the need for a carrier-capable variant of the plane, which is now scheduled to be the third of the three types developed. Instead it could purchase more F/A-18E/F Super Hornets (or refurbish existing F/A-18C/Ds) while awaiting improved UAV technology. The JSF program is experiencing a number of development challenges, such as keeping weight within prescribed limits. At present, that is particularly true for the Marine variant, but such problems could grow, as then Air Force Secretary James Roche recently acknowledged.[53]

The Navy should further pursue its fresh thinking on how to sustain deployments of ships overseas more efficiently and economically. It has reduced its previous emphasis on maintaining continual overseas presence in certain theaters, electing instead to keep more ships in U.S. ports, from which they can surge overseas in larger numbers quickly if needed. The Navy should go further, exploring the idea—developed in part at the Center for Naval Analyses—of keeping ships overseas for longer periods of time and rotating crews by airlift.[54]

This idea should be considered in particular for the Navy's new DDX land-attack destroyer, a ship designed to be an innovative platform, with a stealthier hull shape and materials as well as electric propulsion and a great deal of automation. The combined effects of these new technologies should increase the ship's survivability against hostile fire and permit much smaller crews. The concept is probably smart, but there are risks, including the ship's unusual shape, which has led to some doubts about its seaworthiness. In any event, the ship will be expensive, perhaps approaching $2 billion per vessel despite much more optimistic projections by the Navy.[55]

Rather than purchase the sixteen to twenty-four DDX destroyers the Navy now seems to want, the service could purchase eight instead. It could try to base four overseas—or at least keep four overseas for stretches of roughly two years at a time. That would not impose a huge hardship on the Navy overall, or on its shipbuilders. Having just reached the end of its long purchase run of DDG-51 destroyers, it is also embarking on a concept for a smaller vessel, the littoral combat ship, and aspires to increase the size of the fleet by 20 percent in coming years. In addition, the country has a great deal of firepower from bombers, other aircraft, submarines, and existing ships, making the case for a large purchase of DDX vessels suspect.[56] This approach could save nearly $1 billion a year over the next decade.

In addition, the Navy should explore ways to save money in its nuclear submarine program. It aspires to retain at least fifty-five attack submarines and perhaps a dozen more than that in the future, but in fact it may have trouble keeping forty submarines in the coming years since some classes of subs are aging quickly and budget constraints may limit future procurement.[57] One option is to buy fewer Virginia class subs but to compensate by basing more at Guam—up to a half-dozen, according to a proposal from the Congressional Budget Office. That would preserve the Navy's overall capacity to maintain submarines on forward station, where they are important for intelligence gathering and other missions, particularly in the western Pacific Ocean. Associated savings could exceed $20 billion over the next fifteen to twenty years.[58] The Navy should also consider swapping crews while submarines are forward deployed, permitting a smaller sub fleet.

Even with these changes the Navy would still expand its fleet of major combatants. But rather than increase from 294 to 375 as now hoped, the fleet would number 325 to 350 ships.[59]

Conclusion

A "silver bullet" approach to weapons modernization that emphasized the importance of electronics, sensors, and advanced munitions more than replacing major weapons platforms with systems typically costing twice as much would make maximum use of current trends in technology.[60] It would represent a partial slowdown compared with the timing of current plans, recognizing the considerable U.S. lead over any potential foe and allowing a more patient and selective strategy of modernization. But such an approach would hardly amount to standing still; indeed, it would be designed to emphasize those areas of technology in which the rate of change is fastest and the potential for progress greatest.

This approach would certainly not result in the cancellation of production of all new weapons. Some new high-tech fighters, ships, and ground combat vehicles would be acquired. But some weapons would indeed be canceled, and others would be purchased in significantly fewer numbers than now intended. Certainly, the current Pentagon vision, which largely amounts to the wholesale replacement of existing weapons with next-generation weapons, would be discarded.

To make sure that the military's weaponry remains safe and dependable, existing variants of weapons could be refurbished. Or new copies of technology already in service—like F-16 aircraft and Black Hawk heli-copters—could be built. This overall procurement strategy would hardly be cheap; budgets would, in fact, have to keep rising above current levels of $75 billion or so. But it could save more than $10 billion a year compared with existing Pentagon plans.

SIX

Beyond Iraq and North Korea

The immediate challenge of U.S. defense planning is to manage the current strain on military forces while keeping the defense budget within bounds. It is entirely appropriate that such a difficult task should command the bulk of the time and intellectual resources of U.S. defense strategists today, but it is time to begin to think about what organizing framework the Department of Defense should employ after the intense period of the Iraq operation is over. This concluding chapter sketches out several broad considerations as well as several specific scenarios to help initiate the process.

Among its other implications, this chapter suggests that the U.S. military will need substantial numbers of ground forces even after the Iraq operation is complete; it will also have to retain substantial numbers of advanced air and naval forces. The requisite numbers are unlikely to be any more than today, and perhaps somewhat less. Quite likely, there will be an opportunity to do what the Navy has already begun to do, cutting personnel modestly as it devises more efficient ways of performing various tasks. But the overall message of the analysis in this chapter is one of conservatism. Those who would radically reshape the American armed forces, even in the aftermath of the Iraq operation, may not have given sufficient attention to the wide range of possible and quite demanding scenarios that could threaten U.S. security thereafter. At least two that are quite plausible—involving conflict against North Korea or in the Taiwan Strait—could involve 200,000 or more American forces for months and perhaps even longer. Several others, some of which could continue for years should they ever begin, could involve 30,000 to 50,000 American troops at a time. That would imply a need for forces at least three to four times as large as the number deployed at any moment. And of course, it is entirely conceivable that two of these operations, or even more, could occur over the same period.

U.S. defense planning after the cold war was organized around the possibility of two overlapping wars. This scenario guided the sizing and shaping of the American armed forces under three presidents (both Bushes as well as Clinton) and five secretaries of defense (Cheney, Aspin, Perry, Cohen, and Rumsfeld). Only enough strategic lift was purchased for one war at a time, so the assumption was that the wars would be spaced by at least one to three months but that their durations might overlap, requiring enough combat and support forces as well as munitions and supplies for two effectively simultaneous operations.

There was a broad deterrence logic to the two-war framework: when involved in a future war, which most observers thought quite likely at some point, the United States would not want to invite attacks on its allies or interests abroad. So it would need to be able to respond robustly to a second crisis or conflict while engaged in a major combat operation.

The two-war logic also had a basis in specific, highly possible scenarios. The most plausible enemies were Iraq under Saddam Hussein and North Korea under the Kims. The first Bush administration contemplated a broader range of possible conflicts, including war to protect the Baltic states from a resurgent Russia. But it acknowledged that the two-regional-war scenario was the most demanding.[1] The Clinton administration later reduced the size of the active duty military by about 15 percent of what Bush had planned. It pointed to the greater capabilities of modern weaponry and argued that increased use of prepositioned supplies and equipment as well as fast transport could compensate for smaller armed forces. But it otherwise echoed much of the Bush logic and also emphasized the Iraq and North Korea scenarios.[2] The first Bush and the Clinton administrations both argued that forces designed to handle two regional wars could also address other possible, lesser conflicts.

In 2001, the George W. Bush administration modified the two-war concept somewhat, while keeping much of the basic logic. Specifically, Secretary of Defense Rumsfeld argued that the United States did not need the capacity to win both wars in a decisive fashion (meaning unconditional surrender of the enemy and occupation of its territory) at the same time. In the end, this change in doctrine had only limited implications for force planning, even though Rumsfeld reportedly toyed with the idea of cutting two divisions from the active Army before abandoning the idea.[3]

In the aftermath of the overthrow of Saddam Hussein, further changes are needed in America's armed forces and their undergirding defense strategy. The acute and near-term problem of handling the Iraq occupation is the subject of chapter 3. But even as it is addressed, strategists and planners need to think about what comes next. At some point, Iraq presumably will no longer be one of the two chief objects of U.S military force planning.

The two-war framework should be retained in some form. The deterrent logic of being able to do more than one thing at a time is rock solid. If the United States is involved in one major conflict and perhaps occupied in one or more smaller ongoing operations around the world, it also needs additional capability to deter other crises as well as to maintain forward presence, carry out joint exercises with allies, and handle smaller problems. The current "1-4-2-1" framework for force planning was a good modification of the previous two-war framework. By that approach, the United States prepared to defend the homeland, maintain strong forward deployments in four main theaters (Europe, the Persian Gulf, northeast Asia, and other parts of the Pacific Rim), defeat two regional aggressors at once if necessary, and overthrow one of them.[4] But it was designed principally for a world in which hypothetical wars against Iraq or North Korea could still dominate U.S. defense planning.

The scenarios described in this chapter concern the type of possible operations that defense planners will need to consider in the coming years—if not yet fully in the 2005–06 quadrennial defense review, then certainly by the end of the decade.[5] The Pentagon has recently shifted from "threat-based analysis" to "capabilities-based analysis," meaning that instead of focusing on specific threats, such as Iraq and North Korea, it will instead emphasize the U.S. military capabilities that may be needed for future warfare more generally. But even the latter approach clearly requires some sense of the nature, size, and location of plausible American opponents.

The following discussion begins with Korea and the Taiwan Strait, which it considers in some detail. My overall finding is that, while both are very demanding scenarios, either could be handled with the existing U.S. force structure, at least for a time. Were war in Korea to require an extensive occupation, more drastic policy changes, including full activation of the National Guard and Reserve—or perhaps even a form of military conscription—might be needed. But the forces urgently needed to defeat aggression and defend American allies in either possible conflict should be available, even as the Iraq mission continues.

Given these findings, the Iraq operation can and should continue to be seen as the centerpiece of current U.S. force planning, and the demands of the operation can guide most necessary near-term modifications to the force structure. For that reason this chapter is last in the book, whereas the analysis of the Iraq operation is presented earlier. The chapter concludes with an overview of other scenarios that to date have received less attention. The goal is not to conduct a detailed analysis but rather to sketch out plausible scenarios and to estimate corresponding rough U.S. force requirements.

In the spirit of maintaining as much continuity as possible with previous doctrines, the set of scenarios considered here suggests changing the 1-4-2-1 framework to, perhaps, 1-4-1-1-1. The "4" would be reinterpreted slightly, to refer not only to forward deployments but to limited-scale counterterrorist strikes as well. Viewing it in this light would place clear emphasis on maintaining a diverse global network of military bases and the forward deployments necessary for small but rapid and decisive strikes or other operations. The "1-1-1" would refer to one large-scale stabilization mission (presently in Iraq, of course, but perhaps someday in South or Southeast Asia, the Middle East, or Africa), one high-intensity air-ground war (for example, in Korea), and one major naval-air engagement (such as in the Taiwan Strait or Persian Gulf).

War and Occupation in Korea?

Many at the Pentagon have long believed that by mounting a surprise attack, North Korea could make significant gains in South Korea, quite possibly including the capture of Seoul, before U.S. reinforcements could arrive in sufficient numbers to work with surviving South Korean troops to stop and reverse the onslaught. But given continued improvements in South Korean and U.S. capabilities, together with gradual atrophy of the main combat forces of the Democratic People's Republic of Korea (DPRK), allied prospects for successfully defending Republic of Korea (ROK) territory today appear rather good and are likely to remain that way in the future.

Still, the United States cannot neglect the Korean Peninsula in its war planning and force structure analysis. An escalating crisis over nuclear weapons could lead to war. That could happen if the United States and its allies grow acutely worried that North Korea might sell nuclear materials abroad, or if they decide that Pyongyang must be prevented from developing a large nuclear arsenal. It could also happen if North Korea miscalculates the new leverage its current nuclear capabilities afford it and pushes its brinkmanship too far.[6]

Two main questions arise. One, would a war on the peninsula lead to many hundreds of thousands of military and civilian casualties or might it be won more quickly and decisively using innovative war plans and new technologies? Second, the number of U.S. forces needed for the defense and ultimate liberation of the ROK have been estimated by Pentagon planners at roughly six ground combat divisions, including Marine and Army units, ten wings of Air Force aircraft, and four to five Navy aircraft carrier battle groups—altogether totaling at least a half-million U.S. military personnel. Are those estimates still valid?[7]

First, some background. Although U.S. defense reviews in the 1990s lumped Korea with Southwest Asia conceptually, the peninsula is much more like a cross between the area that existed along the intra-German border and Bosnia than like Kuwait, Saudi Arabia, or southern Iraq. That image applies to both the nature of the terrain and the nature of the fighting forces deployed in the vicinity. Indeed, the Korean peninsula remains the most densely militarized region on Earth, where North Korean forces of about 1 million (with a defense budget that may exceed 25 percent of GDP and even approach 40 percent) face off against combined allied forces of about 600,000.[8] The Korean peninsula as a whole is roughly 250 kilometers wide at its narrowest point and about 1,000 kilometers long. It is characterized by very hilly topography; much of what flat land exists is marsh or rice fields.

Significantly more than 1 million troops and 20,000 armored vehicles or artillery pieces—as well as more than 1 million land mines, abundant chemical weapons, and fortified defensive positions—are found between Pyongyang and Seoul. (The distance from the four-kilometer-wide demilitarized zone (DMZ) to Seoul is roughly forty kilometers and that from the DMZ to Pyongyang is about 125 kilometers.) Forces in Korea are more densely concentrated than Warsaw Pact and NATO units were in Central Europe during the cold war. For North Korea, in fact, roughly 65 percent of its total units and up to 80 percent of its estimated aggregate firepower are within 100 kilometers of the DMZ, significantly greater percentages than in the 1980s.[9]

There exist only two main natural axes of potential attack in the (relatively) flat western part of the peninsula, near Seoul. Known as the Chorwon and Munsan corridors, each is about fifteen kilometers wide in some places, and they branch out and interconnect in others. Another three to four attack corridors could be imagined in the central and eastern parts of the country, given the existing road networks and terrain, although the coastal route along the Sea of Japan (known in Korea as the East Sea) would be the most easily accessed by vehicles.[10]

North Korea would probably begin any war with a massive artillery barrage of South Korean and U.S. positions below the DMZ, and likely of Seoul itself. Chemical weapons might well be used. Infantry and mechanized forces would then try to take advantage of the carnage and chaos to penetrate U.S.-ROK defenses and reach Seoul quickly. They would be aided by about 100,000 special forces, some predeployed in South Korea if possible, that would move by tunnels, small planes, mini-submarines, and more conventional means. North Korea would probably try to catch the allies by surprise, profit from cloud cover that would reduce (somewhat) the effectiveness of U.S. airpower, and seize Seoul before U.S. reinforcements (or South Korean reserve soldiers) could arrive en masse. It then might try to take the rest of the peninsula; more likely, perhaps, given its limited capability for long-range mechanized movement, it might try to use Seoul as a hostage to negotiate a favorable political settlement.[11]

Given this background, do the United States and South Korea have the capacity to wage a robust defensive and then a timely, decisive, offensive war against North Korea? And what forces would they need if war should occur?

Preemptive use of force by the ROK and the United States against North Korea seems very unlikely. Even though there may be ways to win a war in Korea faster than is commonly assumed, the carnage would likely be great whatever period of time the war endured, for several reasons. First, so many North Korean weapons are positioned near Seoul, many in protected locations, that even a well-timed surprise attack could not prevent thousands of explosive rounds launched by artillery tube or missile from landing in Seoul.[12]

Second, many North Korean military and political headquarters are deep underground, making it hard to attack them even with a "shock and awe" type of air campaign. U.S. special forces would also have a harder time infiltrating North Korea and locating such sites for aerial attack than in Iraq, given the degree to which the country is cut off from outsiders.

Third, there is no easy axis of approach to Pyongyang similar to the open desert that coalition forces used in their race to Baghdad in March and April of 2003. The terrain in Korea is difficult and complex. Among other implications, that means that enemy harassment of supply lines, which coalition forces faced at only a few specific sites in Operation Iraqi Freedom, could be a much more pervasive problem in any invasion of North Korea.

Fourth, North Korea's military, with a total active duty strength of more than (or at least near) 1 million, is much larger than Iraq's. Fifth, North Korean troops are believed to be even more thoroughly indoctrinated by their leadership, and hence more dedicated to their nation's defense, than were Saddam's forces, three-fourths of whom were believed unlikely to fight hard before the war began (an expectation that appears to have been roughly correct). Few observers make a similar assumption about North Korea's military.[13] Reportedly many North Koreans made it their first priority to salvage pictures of the Dear Leader—whether out of loyalty or fear—when a train explosion in the spring of 2004 caused huge damage and many casualties in a northwestern DPRK city.

Similar conclusions follow for North Korea's top military and political leaders, who would probably fight on even if somehow Kim Jong Il were killed in a "decapitation attack" of the type attempted against Saddam Hussein at the beginning of Operation Iraqi Freedom.[14] It is for these reasons that war simulations, even if inexact, predict hundreds of thousands of deaths in any future Korean war regardless of how it might start. The simulations may be exaggerations of likely casualties—but by a factor of two or three, not ten or twenty.

The last two arguments in particular have another set of implications. They mean that, in all likelihood, winning decisively in Korea would require hundreds of thousands of U.S. troops in addition to the large ROK armed forces. It is worth reexamining the details of the war plan more rigorously than is possible here. But an initial assessment suggests that existing force requirements may not be far off. Fortunately, in North Korea any invasion would be followed by an occupation that the South Korean armed forces could probably handle largely on their own (unlike the situation in Iraq). But that invasion phase itself could be difficult—and it would be very important to keep it as short as possible, given the astronomically large numbers of casualties that would accumulate with each added day of fighting. The Pentagon's official estimate that at least half a million military personnel could be needed for such a war may be too conservative. But if the overall Iraq experience is any guide, its conservatism is probably best estimated as in the range of 10 to 20 percent excess manpower, not 50 percent or more.

A China-Taiwan War

It seems extremely unlikely that the PRC could seize Taiwan in an amphibious assault, now or anytime in the foreseeable future, for many reasons: its strategic lift is inadequate; its top-line equipment is limited in quantity (see table 6-1); Taiwan's defenses are extensive; modern sensors (Taiwanese and American) make the possibility of true surprise attack remote; and precision weapons make it harder than ever for large transports like ships and airplanes to succeed in a major assault.[15]

Table 6-1. *Basic Military Data for the United States, China, and Taiwan, 2003*[a]

Type of military capability	China	Taiwan	United States
Population	1.3 billion	22.6 million	290 million
Active duty military personnel	2.26 million	290,000	1.44 million
Reserve personnel	800,000	1.66 million	876,000
Active Army and Marines	1.6 million	200,000	678,000
Active Air Force	400,000	45,000	375,000
Active Navy	255,000	45,000	384,000
Annual defense spending ($2005)	56.7 billion	$6.7 billion	$410.6 billion
Heavy armor, including tanks, armored personnel carriers, large artillery	28,300	4,500	31,700
Combat jets (number of advanced jets)	2,600 (154)	511 (331)	2,268 (2,268)
Major ships (number of aircraft carriers)	63 (0)	32 (0)	125 (12)
Attack submarines (number of advanced subs)	69 (6)	4 (0)	54 (54)
Nuclear weapons	402	0	7,088

Source: For the population of China and Taiwan, see Department of State (www.state.gov/r/ pa/ei/bgn/ [April 29, 2004]). See International Institute for Strategic Studies, *The Military Balance 2004/2005* (Oxford University Press, 2004), p. 353, for China's publicly reported annual defense spending; p. 251 for China's nuclear weapons stockpile; and pp. 170–73 for all other Chinese categories. For Taiwan's annual defense spending, see International Institute for Strategic Studies, *The Military Balance 2004/2005*, p. 353; for all other Taiwanese categories, see pp. 189–90. For 2003 reserve personnel, see "Prepared Testimony of U.S. Secretary of Defense Donald H. Rumsfeld," Senate Armed Services Committee, February 3, 2004, p. 6 (www.senate.gov/~armed_services/ statemnt/2004/February/Rumsfeld.pdf [March 10, 2004]). For total active duty military personnel—Army and Marines, Air Force, and Navy—as of August 31, 2003, see Department of Defense, Directorate for Information Operations and Reports, "Active Duty Military Personnel by Service by Rank/Grade" (web1.whs.osd.mil/ mmid/military/rg0308.pdf [April 29, 2004]). For American annual defense spending, see International Institute for Strategic Studies, *The Military Balance 2004/2005*, p. 353. For American heavy armor, see International Institute for Strategic Studies, *The Military Balance 2004/2005*, p. 24. For American combat jets, see "USAF Almanac," *Air Force Magazine*, May 2003, pp. 82. For American aircraft carriers, major ships, and attack submarines, see "United States Navy Fact File" (www.chinfo.navy.mil/navpalib/factfile/ffiletop.html [April 13, 2004]). For American nuclear weapons, see International Institute for Strategic Studies, *The Military Balance 2004/2005*, p. 251.

a. Actual PRC military spending could be as high as $65 billion, according to the Department of Defense, *Annual Report on the Military Power of the People's Republic of China*, July 28, 2003. The number of nuclear weapons includes both strategic and tactical nuclear weapons.

Even if China could not seize Taiwan, it could try to use military force in a more limited way to pressure Taipei to accept terms for political association that would be highly favorable to Beijing. Two scenarios are of particular interest: a missile attack designed to terrorize or coerce, and a blockade. In the latter case at least, U.S. military forces would probably need to come to Taiwan's aid in order to avoid slow strangulation of the island.[16]

Consider first a possible missile attack by China against Taiwan. The PRC had some 500 ballistic missiles deployed near Taiwan as of 2004.[17] From their current positions, the M-9 and M-11 missiles can reach Taiwan, but neither possesses sufficient accuracy to strike military assets effectively using conventional explosives. Indeed, they would generally miss their targets by several football fields and almost always by the length of at least a single field. Granted, if Beijing unleashed a salvo of hundreds of missiles, it might register a few direct hits against lucrative military targets (as well as dozens of hits, with varying degrees of lethality, against population centers). Commercial sea traffic might diminish drastically for a period of time. But if China exhausted the bulk of its missile inventory to sink a grand total of two or three cargo vessels and temporarily slow operations at a port or an airfield, that might not be seen as such an intimidating or successful use of force.

The more troubling coercive scenario is a blockade. Rather than relying on sheer terror and intimidation, it could take aim at Taiwan's economy and try to drag it down substantially for an indefinite period. It is doubtful that China could truly cut Taiwan off from the outside world with such a blockade. However, if willing to take losses, it could certainly take a toll on commercial ships trading with Taiwan as well as Taiwanese military forces trying to break the blockade, driving up the cost of insuring any vessels that subsequently still sought to carry goods to and from the island. In all likelihood, China could not quarantine Taiwan.[18] But even with an imperfect, "leaky" blockade, it could sink enough commercial ships to scare others off, and do so over an extended period. Should it convince most commercial shippers not to risk trips to Taiwan, it could effectively begin to strangle the island. If Beijing then offered Taiwan a compromise, Taipei might be coerced into capitulation. For example, Beijing might demand reaffirmation of the one-China principle and some degree of political fealty from Taiwan while permitting the island to retain autonomous rule, an independent economy, and perhaps some armed forces. Moreover, whether Taipei could be coerced in this way or not, China might believe that it could—and hence try such coercive use of force in response to any future behavior from Taipei that it finds unacceptable.[19]

A Chinese blockade could take a number of forms. But for the PRC, the least risky and most natural approach would simply be to attempt to introduce significant risk in all maritime voyages in and out of Taiwan by occasionally sinking a cargo ship with submarines or with mines laid in Taiwan's harbors. China does not have aircraft carriers to help with a blockade and is unlikely to for years to come.[20] Using airplanes and surface ships would put more of its own forces at risk, especially since it could not realistically hope to eliminate Taipei's air force with a preemptive attack. It would also be a rather straightforward matter for the United States to quickly defeat a blockade that used planes and surface ships. So a submarine attack would be most likely. China might couple such a blockade with a preemptive air and special forces attack—but perhaps just a limited strike focused on Taiwanese submarine-hunting ships and airplanes, which it might be able to attack effectively.

Most of China's submarines do not at present have antiship cruise missiles or great underwater endurance,[21] and their capacity to conduct a coordinated blockade operation in conjunction with surface and aerial assets is limited.[22] However, those shortcomings may not be particularly onerous when the submarines' targets are commercial ships approaching Taiwan. The submarines have adequate range on a single tank of fuel— typically almost 10,000 miles—to stay deployed east of Taiwan for substantial periods.[23] Although their ability to coordinate with each other and reconnaissance aircraft is limited, that might not matter greatly for the purposes of a "leaky" blockade. Carrying torpedoes with a range of ten kilometers or more and picking up commercial ships by sonar or by sight, individual submarines could maintain patrol over a large number of the sea approaches to Taiwan.[24] It could take Taiwan weeks to find the better PRC submarines, particularly if China used them in a hit-and-run mode. Modern attack submarines are able to detect enemy warships at considerable distance, and they are fast when submerged (unlike the case, say, in World War II); those capabilities give them a chance to escape ships without exposing themselves on the surface.[25]

Taiwan could use its surface fleet to organize and accompany convoys of merchant ships. However, it would be harder to do that for ships approaching Taiwan than for those leaving, since approaching ships come from many different places—and if they assembled east of Taiwan to wait for escorts they would be vulnerable at that point. An additional complication is that Chinese submarines lucky enough to be lying quietly in wait in the right places would tend to hear approaching convoys before they were themselves detected, making it likely that they could get off the first shot—if not the first couple of shots—before putting themselves at risk.

The overall outcome of such a struggle is very hard to predict. China's advanced submarine force is small, but Taiwan's advanced antisubmarine warfare capabilities are not much greater. Uncertainties also exist over how many escort ships Taiwan would lose in a preemptive Chinese attack and over how proficiently the two sides would use their respective assets.[26] Whatever the dynamics, Taiwan probably could not neutralize China's submarines very quickly.

Chinese mines would likely pose a problem too. China's submarines usually carry two to three dozen mines each, so half of its entire submarine fleet would carry about 1,000. If half the fleet was able to deploy mines near Taiwan without being sunk, China would be able to deploy nearly as many mines as Iraq did—with considerable effect—against the U.S.-led coalition in 1990–91. Moreover, China surely has, and will acquire, more sophisticated mines than Iraq possessed, including "smart mines" that would be difficult for minehunters to find and neutralize.[27] Moreover, Taiwan's minesweeping ships are limited in number and mediocre in quality and condition. It is likely that China could exact a price with its mines, perhaps causing attrition rates of several percent each time ships tried to enter or leave Taiwan's ports.[28]

The U.S. Military Steps In

For the above reasons, American military intervention might be needed to protect Taiwan and its economy. The basic approach would be for U.S. antisubmarine operations to set up a safe shipping lane east of Taiwan and near Taiwanese ports. To carry out that mission, the United States, together with Taiwan, would need to establish air superiority, protect ships against Chinese submarine attack, and cope with the threat of mines.

One forward antisubmarine warfare (ASW) barrier could be maintained by U.S. attack submarines operating in the Taiwan Strait, most probably near China's ports. That would be the first line of defense. Those submarines would seek to destroy any Chinese submarines they found, and over time they could decimate the PRC submarine force, except perhaps for those vessels that remained in port throughout the conflict.

The second ASW barrier would consist of ships, primarily ASW frigates, accompanying convoys of merchant ships as they sailed in from the open ocean east of Taiwan. These convoys might form a thousand miles or more east of Taiwan, enjoying armed protection from that point onward as they traveled to the island and later as they departed. The frigates would listen for approaching submarines and for the sound of any torpedoes being fired, and aircraft carriers would provide the ships with air cover.

Finally, additional assets would be dedicated to various special purposes. Some would protect U.S. aircraft carriers; others would provide additional protection to ships, whether merchant ships or mine warfare vessels, as they operated near Taiwan's shores and thus fairly close to China. Two main types of assets might be used. Surface ships—either additional frigates or SURTASS arrays towed by T-AGOS vessels—might be deployed near aircraft carrier battle groups to provide additional protection for those groups. In addition, P-3 aircraft could be kept on call or airborne to pursue any submarines that might be roughly localized by ship or submarine sonar. U.S. minehunters and minesweepers would, of course, operate near Taiwan's ports and the main approaches to those ports. Land- or ship-based helicopters would assist them, as might robotic submersibles deployed from ships near shore.

The U.S. aircraft carrier battle groups would operate east of Taiwan. They would probably function best as two pairs. One pair would be stationed relatively near the island to ensure air superiority over and around Taiwan. Another pair would operate well east of the island, serving in part as a backup for the pair near Taiwan. In addition, they would provide control of the airspace over the open ocean east of Taiwan, helping to defend against any indirect Chinese attack (most likely by longer-range bombers) that managed to avoid the first pair of carriers and Taiwan's air force.

As an alternative to one or two of the carriers, several squadrons of U.S. Air Force or Navy aircraft might be deployed on Taiwan, provided that hardened shelters, effective air defense, and logistical support for them could be made available there. If most of Taiwan's air force survived initial Chinese attacks, that alternative might not be deemed desirable in some circumstances, given concerns about overcrowding airfields and flight corridors. But it would be a sound option to consider in order to reduce strain on the Navy's carrier battle groups and provide for shorter fighter flight paths to the waters of the Taiwan Strait. It could also be important in preparing any offensive options that might be considered at some point against nearby coastal regions of the PRC mainland (for example, ports, ships, and airfields near Taiwan). In addition, it could be helpful to station some surveillance and support aircraft, such as AWACS, JSTARS, and tankers, on Taiwan. Finally, if Japan allowed it—hardly a given—U.S. aircraft at Kadena air base on Okinawa could contribute to the operation as well, securing the northern flank of the theater of operations. Overall, in any event, these missions would not tax the U.S. Air Force nearly as much as the operation might tax the Navy.

My estimates, detailed elsewhere, suggest that the United States would need a force of more than 100,000 to help break a Chinese blockade.[29] It would require few if any ground forces, but perhaps 25 to 50 percent more naval capability than commonly assumed for a major theater conflict. Depending on the availability of bases, substantial Air Force combat capability, reconnaissance capability, and personnel could be needed in theater as well—with basing on Guam, perhaps in Japan, and quite possibly on Taiwan too. The Air Force capabilities required would likely be less than for a major theater war of the classic, post–cold war variety, but they could total half as many.

The outcome of such an engagement would almost assuredly favor the United States and Taiwan eventually, assuming no nuclear escalation. But there is debate about the likely losses that would result. Some have argued that a dozen or more American ships could be sunk by the Chinese submarine force, which will add at least eight modern vessels in the coming years, and by other PRC capabilities. My own estimates are lower and assume that the United States could devise tactics to profit from the limited range and endurance of diesel submarines, as well as the relatively deeper and more sonar-friendly waters east of Taiwan. Such tactics could force PRC submarines to move about and thereby reveal their locations. Until then, shipping would be vulnerable, but if the PRC attacked Taiwanese vessels during that time, its submarines would have to reveal their positions, thereby facing much greater risk.[30]

New Military Scenarios

Just as the Afghanistan war surprised almost everyone in the defense community, other scenarios that have not been frequently analyzed may arise. Several of these are in the category of large-scale stabilization operations.[31] At least one other possibility, war against Iran in the Persian Gulf, could have some similarities to a conflict in the Taiwan Strait. All are offered here as a catalyst for further thinking and analysis rather than as complete assessments in themselves.

Stabilizing and Reforming a Palestinian State?

With Mideast peace elusive, some have gone back to the drawing board to devise new approaches to negotiating a settlement. Someday, leaders in Israel and the Palestinian territories may be willing to return to the 2000 Clinton administration process and work out an accord based on the classic land-for-peace logic. But it is at least as plausible, even in post-Arafat Palestine, that the violence will continue, that many Palestinian groups will find it difficult to accept any peace deal that endorses Israel's right to exist, and that Israel itself will show little interest in a deal at least until the threat of terrorism can be addressed.

It is beyond the scope of this monograph to address the diplomatic creativity that breaking this logjam might require. But it could also require a military component, which could well entail deployment of an international force in the Palestinian territories, assuming circumstances under which the Palestinian Authority invites such a force into its territory (perhaps as part of a deal recognizing its sovereignty, even as the authority in effect immediately surrenders part of that sovereignty to the outside force). The multinational coalition would deploy troops partly along the frontiers with Israel, but also as an internal security force to help stabilize Palestinian territory and reform its security units to reduce the influence of extremist elements. American forces would likely have to play a substantial role in any such mission. This idea may seem implausible to some now, but it has been suggested by Martin Indyk, former U.S. ambassador to

Israel and assistant secretary of state, as one of the few ways that the current Palestinian-Israeli impasse might be addressed.[32]

Any security force in Palestinian territory would have the advantage of dealing with a small population in a small geographic area. But it would face the disadvantages of dealing with numerous militias and terrorist groups in urban settings, making law enforcement and counterinsurgency operations quite difficult.

The population of the West Bank and Gaza is roughly 3.5 million. Palestinians have a per-capita average annual income of somewhat less than $1,000, although actual economic circumstances are perhaps worse than those figures suggest since unemployment is rampant. Official security forces number about 30,000. Various militias and terrorist groups have an estimated combined strength of perhaps 5,000.[33]

Given these parameters, what might an operation in Palestinian territory entail? The first order of business would be to ensure deployment of a force that is both large enough and has the training necessary to help in policing and stabilizing the country. Basic rules of thumb suggest that the necessary forces should total 1,000 to 10,000 troops or police officers for every 1 million inhabitants. But in Palestine, given the stakes involved and the history of violence, the upper end of the range seems more plausible. Indeed, the density of international forces in Kosovo was greater—up to 20,000 personnel for every million Kosovars—and that density might be needed in Palestinian territory as well. Overall, circumstances require perhaps 20,000 to 50,000 foreign forces, of which anywhere from 15 to 50 percent could be American. Prudent planning suggests that U.S. numerical force requirements might total 10,000 to 20,000 personnel for five to ten years.

These forces would need to be ready for a difficult time ahead. They would be recruiting, vetting, and training a new Palestinian security force while gradually ensuring the dismantling and disarming of existing groups. Opposition could be expected, and it could be violent at times. The border with Israel would need to be vigilantly monitored. The job would take years and could involve at least dozens of American casualties. After the ongoing Iraq mission, it could seem relatively easy, but it would not be easy in any absolute sense.

Preventing Nuclear Catastrophe in South Asia

Of all the military scenarios short of a direct threat to its territory that would undoubtedly involve the vital interests of the United States, the collapse of Pakistan ranks very high on the list. The combination of Islamic extremists and nuclear weapons that exists in the country is extremely worrisome; if parts of Pakistan's nuclear arsenal ever fall into the wrong hands, al Qaeda could conceivably gain access to a nuclear device, with terrifying possible results. Another quite worrisome South Asia scenario would involve another confrontation between India and Pakistan over Kashmir, possibly leading to all-out war between these two nuclear-armed states.[34]

The Pakistani collapse scenario appears unlikely given Pakistan's relatively pro-Western and secular officer corps.[35] But the intelligence services, which created the Taliban and have condoned if not abetted Islamic extremists in Kashmir, are less dependable. And the country as a whole is sufficiently infiltrated by fundamentalist groups—as the assassination attempts against President Musharraf as well as other evidence make clear—that this terrifying scenario of civil chaos cannot be entirely dismissed.[36]

Were it to occur, it is unclear what the United States and like-minded states would or should do. It is very unlikely that "surgical strikes" could be conducted to destroy the nuclear weapons before extremists could make a grab for them. It is doubtful that the United States would know their location and at least as doubtful that any Pakistani government would countenance such a move, even under duress.

If a surgical strike, series of surgical strikes, or commando-style raids were not possible, the only option might be to try to quell the unrest before the weapons could be taken by extremists and transferred to terrorists. The United States and other outside powers might, for example, respond to a request by the Pakistani government to help restore order. But given the embarrassment associated with requesting outside help, the request might not be made until it was almost too late, complicating the task of putting down the insurrection before nuclear arsenals could be threatened. Hence such an operation would be extremely demanding, but there might be little choice about whether to attempt it. The international community, if it could act fast enough, might help defeat an insurrection.

Or it might help protect Pakistan's borders, making it hard to sneak nuclear weapons out of the country, while providing only technical support to the Pakistani armed forces as they tried to put down the insurrection. The only certainty is that, given the enormous stakes, the United States would literally have to do anything it could to prevent nuclear weapons from getting into the wrong hands.

Should stabilization efforts be required, the scale of the undertaking could be breathtaking. Pakistan is a very large country. Its population is just under 150 million, six times Iraq's. Its land area is roughly twice that of Iraq; its perimeter is about 50 percent longer. Stabilizing a country of that size could easily require several times as many troops as the Iraq mission—with a figure of up to 1 million being plausible.

Of course, any international force would have help. Presumably some fraction of Pakistan's security forces would remain intact, able, and willing to help defend the country. Pakistan's military numbers 550,000 army troops, 70,000 uniformed personnel in the air force and navy, another 510,000 reservists, and almost 300,000 gendarmes and Interior Ministry troops.[37] But if some substantial fraction of the military, say one-quarter to one-third, broke off from the main body and were assisted by extremist militias, it is quite possible that the international community would need to deploy 100,000 to 200,000 troops to ensure quick restoration of order. Given the need for rapid response, the U.S. share of this total would probably be a majority fraction, or quite possibly 50,000 to 100,000 ground forces.

What about the scenario of war between Pakistan and India over Kashmir? It is highly doubtful that the United States would ever wish to actively take sides in such a conflict, allying with one country to defeat the other. Its interests in the matter of who controls Kashmir are not great enough to justify such intervention, and no formal alliance commitments oblige it to step in. Moreover, the military difficulty of the operation would be extreme, in light of the huge armed forces arrayed on the subcontinent and the inland location and complex topography of Kashmir. In addition to the numbers cited above for Pakistan, India's armed forces number 1.3 million active duty troops and possess such assets as 4,000 tanks, nineteen submarines, and about 750 combat aircraft (the defense budgets of the two countries are $2.5 billion and $13 billion, respectively).[38]

However, there are other ways in which foreign forces might become involved. If India and Pakistan were on the verge of using nuclear weapons, or perhaps had even used them, they might consider what was previously unthinkable, to New Delhi in particular—asking the international community for help. For example, in an accord akin to the Palestine trusteeship idea outlined earlier, they might agree to allow the international community to run Kashmir for a period of years. After a local government was built up and security services reformed, elections might be held to determine the region's future political affiliation, leading to an eventual end to the trusteeship. While this scenario is admittedly highly demanding—and also unlikely in light of India's adamant objections to international involvement in the Kashmir issue—it would be hard to dismiss such an approach out of hand if it seemed to be the only alternative to nuclear war on the subcontinent. Not only could such a war have horrendous human consequences—killing many tens of millions—and shatter the tradition of non-use of nuclear weapons that is so essential to global stability today, but it could also lead to the collapse of Pakistan, thus giving rise to the same type of worries discussed earlier about its nuclear weapons falling into the wrong hands.

What might a stabilization mission in Kashmir entail? The region has about twice the population of Bosnia, and it is half the size of Iraq in population and land area. That suggests an initial stabilization force in the general range of 100,000, with the U.S. contribution perhaps 30,000 to 50,000. The mission would make sense only if India and Pakistan truly blessed it, so there would be little point in deploying a force large enough to hold its own against a concerted attack by one of the two countries. But robust monitoring of border regions against terrorist infiltration, as well as capable counterinsurgent and counterterrorist strike forces, would be necessary.

Stabilizing a Large Country Such as Indonesia or Congo

Consider the possibility of severe unrest in one of the world's large countries, such as Indonesia or Congo or Nigeria. At present, such problems are generally seen as of secondary strategic importance to the United States. Washington may support and help fund a peacekeeping mission under some circumstances but will rarely commit troops—and certainly will not mount a muscular intervention.

However, that state of affairs could change. For example, if al Qaeda developed a major stronghold in a given large country, the United States might consider overthrowing the country's government or helping the government reclaim control of the part of its territory occupied by the terrorists. Or it might intervene to help one side in a civil war against another. For example, if the schism between the police and armed forces in Indonesia worsened and one of the two institutions wound up working with an al Qaeda offshoot, the United States might accept an invitation from the responsible half of the government to help defeat the other and the terrorist organization in question.[39] Or if a terrorist organization were tolerated in Indonesia, the United States might strike at it directly. That could occur if the terrorist group took control of land near a major shipping lane in the Indonesian Straits, or simply if it decided to use part of Indonesia for sanctuary.[40]

Clearly, the requirement for foreign forces would be a function of how much of the country in question became unstable, how intact the indigenous security forces were, and how large any militia or insurgent group proved to be. For illustrative purposes, if a large fraction of Indonesia or all of Congo were to become ungovernable, the operation could be two to three times the scale of the Iraq mission. It could be five times the scale of Iraq if it involved trying to restore order throughout Nigeria, though such an operation could be so daunting that a more limited form of intervention seems more plausible—such as trying to stabilize areas where major ethnic or religious groups come into direct contact.

General guidelines for force planning for such scenarios would suggest the need for roughly 100,000 to 200,000 foreign troops, not unlike the scenario of a collapsing or fracturing Pakistan. For such missions, which would be somewhat less urgent than those considered in South Asia, U.S. contributions might only be 20 to 30 percent of the total. But even so, up to two to three American divisions could be required.

Contending with a Coup in Saudi Arabia

How should the United States respond if a coup, presumably fundamentalist in nature, overthrows the royal family in Saudi Arabia? Such an event would raise the specter of major disruption in the global oil economy. Saudi Arabia, along with the United States and Russia, is one of the world's big three oil producers (in the range of 9 million barrels of oil a day), and it is the largest oil exporter (7 million barrels per day, about 20 percent of the world total). It also has by far the world's largest estimated oil reserves (260 billion barrels, nearly one-quarter of the world total).[41] A sustained cutoff in Saudi oil production would wreak havoc in the world economy.

A coup in Saudi Arabia would raise other worries, some even worse, including the harrowing possibility of the Saudis' pursuit of nuclear weapons. Intensified funneling of Saudi funds to al Qaeda and the madrassas in countries such as Pakistan would also likely result. This type of scenario has been discussed for at least two decades and remains of concern today—perhaps of even greater concern than before, given the surge of terrorist violence in Saudi Arabia in recent years as well as the continued growth and hostile ideology of al Qaeda, along with the broader Wahhabi movement.

What military scenarios might require consideration in such circumstances? If a fundamentalist regime came to power and became interested in acquiring nuclear weapons, the United States might have to consider carrying out forcible regime change. If by contrast the regime was more intent on disrupting the oil economy, more limited measures such as seizing the oil fields might be adequate. Indeed, it might be feasible not to do anything at first, in the hope that the new regime would gradually realize the benefits of reintegrating Saudi Arabia at least partially into the global oil economy. But in the end the United States and other Western countries might consider using force. That could happen, for example, if the new regime refused over a long period to pump oil, or worse yet if it began destroying the oil infrastructure and damaging the oil wells on its territory—perhaps out of a fundamentalist commitment to a return to the lifestyle of the first millenium. Since virtually all Saudi oil is in the eastern coastal zones or in Saudi territorial waters in the Persian Gulf, a military mission to protect and operate the oil wells would have a geographic specificity and finiteness to it. The United States and its partners might then put the proceeds from oil sales into escrow for a future Saudi government that was prepared to make good use of them.

Saudi Arabia has a population nearly as large as Iraq's—some 21 million—and it is more than four times the geographic size of Iraq. Its military numbers 125,000, including 75,000 army troops, as well as another 75,000 personnel in the national guard. But it is not clear whether many of these military units would remain intact in the aftermath of a successful fundamentalist coup—or on which side of any future war they would choose to fight, should a U.S.-led outside force intervene.

Some rough rules of thumb are in order for sizing the requirements for this type of mission. Eastern Saudi Arabia is not heavily populated, but there do exist several mid-sized population centers in the coastal oil zone.[42] About 10,000 to 20,000 foreign troops could be required for policing the 1 million or so people living in that region. Ensuing troop demands would not be inordinate.

However, requirements could be much greater to the extent that a robust defensive perimeter needed to be maintained against incursions by guerrillas. There is no good rule for sizing forces on the basis of the amount of territory to defend. The classic rule—that one division is needed for roughly every 25 kilometers—is clearly too pessimistic.[43] Indeed, no more than several brigades of American forces ultimately secured most of the 350 miles of supply lines in Iraq, which passed through a number of populated regions and significant cities.[44] So a modern American division, patrolling an open area and making use of modern sensors and aircraft, could surely cover 100 to 200 miles of front.

Putting these missions together might imply a total of some three American divisions plus support for a sustained operation to secure the coastal regions of Saudi Arabia. The total force might include 100,000 to 150,000 personnel.

An operation to overthrow a new regime and gradually stabilize a country the size of Saudi Arabia would probably require in the vicinity of 300,000 troops, using standard sizing criteria.

Protecting Persian Gulf Shipping against Iran

In the 1980s, during the war between Iran and Iraq, the United States had to cope with threats to shipping in the Persian Gulf. To ensure the viability of the global oil economy, it reflagged some oil tankers under its own colors and enhanced its naval presence in the region.

This type of scenario could recur. But next time, it could do so in a more worrisome way. Given the ongoing state of tension in U.S.-Iranian relations over matters such as Iran's support for terrorism, Iran's apparent pursuit of nuclear capability, and President Bush's preemption doctrine, any spark could ignite war. Moreover, Iran is not nearly as weak as it was in the late 1980s, when it had spent the better part of a decade fighting Iraq. And since that time, while Iran's arms imports have not increased as fast as some had feared, they have permitted Iran to improve its capacity to threaten shipping lanes in the narrow waters of the Gulf and the Strait of Hormuz. In particular, it has been improving its military capabilities in the very areas that could cause the United States greatest concern—advanced mines, quiet diesel submarines, and precision-guided anti-ship missiles.[45]

This hypothetical worry could become acute, for example, if in the coming years Israel or the United States attacked the exposed parts of Iran's nuclear infrastructure. In such an event, the United States might reinforce its defensive position in the region in advance; alternatively, an aggressive Iranian response against American friends and allies in the region, or against oil tankers in the Persian Gulf, could require a response.

There are two main ways to envision protecting the shipping lanes in question. Either way, a certain number of naval vessels would be needed for antisubmarine warfare, for convoy escort, for minehunting, and for short-range ballistic missile defense. The earlier estimates for the China-Taiwan scenario are roughly indicative of the force requirements here, given the somewhat similar geography. Although the narrowness of the Persian Gulf makes the mission more difficult, Iran is less powerful than China, making the mission overall somewhat easier.

Aerial and sea reconnaissance, as well as quick-strike capabilities, would be needed. Submarines would probably be desired to keep constant track of Iranian submarines. And, of course, ships to protect convoys would likely be required as well. The quantitative requirements for these various assets would be a function of three main factors: geography, rotational policies, and total Iranian force strength. The United States and any allies would need to maintain robust quick-action capabilities along the whole length of the Gulf. They would need to be able to sustain coverage twenty-four hours a day. And, if necessary, they would need to be able to face down an all-out Iranian assault as well.

These sizing criteria lead to the following rough requirements. Given Iran's small submarine force, with just three vessels, probably not more than twenty U.S. submarines would be required (allowing for up to two U.S. subs per Iranian submarine as well as the need to rotate American subs). To ensure continual airspace dominance in the Gulf, roughly as many planes could be required as were needed to enforce the northern and southern no-fly zones over Iraq from 1991 to 2003—some 200 planes in all. Ideally the aircraft would be based at several locations along the 500-mile length of the Gulf to minimize time wasted in transit and to allow for rapid reinforcement should Iran attempt an assault. Some additional number of planes might be needed to establish superiority against Iran's air force, which numbers about 300 planes total, of which perhaps 200 are airworthy.[46] All in all, two aircraft carriers and several squadrons of land-based aircraft could be needed.

Enough surveillance aircraft would be needed to maintain orbits at the northern and southern ends of the Gulf, making for a total of eight to ten planes for air monitoring and a similar number for sea surveillance. If points on the Arabian peninsula were potential targets, in addition to its convoy escorts the United States might need to create a "fence" of ships spaced every fifty to 100 miles along Iran's seacoast to ensure short enough reaction times to counter any launch of ballistic missiles. In addition to a dozen or more ships for such purposes, ten to twenty might escort convoys.

Taken together, the above assets resemble the air and naval components of what has commonly been considered a one-war force package in recent times. Whether some ground forces would be needed as a prudent deterrent against overland Iranian aggression would also have to be considered, but the numbers here would presumably not have to reach the magnitude of those envisioned for a major theater war.

Conclusion

In planning for the future, it is important to bring an open mind and imagination to the task of trying to envision possible military scenarios. The United States typically does not predict its next enemy very well, as evidenced by Operation Desert Storm and even more vividly by the recent war in Afghanistan. So it is important not to lapse into rote answers to the question of which war or major stabilization effort U.S. armed forces may have to wage next.

This is not to advocate pure capabilities-based planning, however. Scenario planning is still needed. The United States needs to develop a rough idea of whom it might fight, where, and over what stakes. Capabilities-based planning is fine once the range of plausible scenarios has been at least somewhat narrowed and specified.

Some threats are implausible. A Russian threat to Europe is now in this category, given the demise of communist ideology and Russia's need for economic interaction with the West. So is the need for American forces to respond to a possible Chinese threat against Siberia and its natural riches. Admittedly, if Russia were to join NATO someday, the United States might theoretically assume an Article V commitment to help guarantee its security against any and all possible threats. On the other hand, NATO is a European-oriented organization, not a Siberian-oriented one. Moreover, it is not necessary and does not make strategic sense for the United States to defend against a hypothetical Chinese overland threat to the Asian landmass. Even a Chinese overland threat to Korea seems extremely unlikely and probably not a sound scenario for force planning purposes.

A war involving invasion of Iran, a country of more than 70 million with a complex geography, is a borderline case. It would be extremely challenging militarily, as American analysts who briefly examined the scenario in the mid-1990s apparently concluded as well, and highly undesirable politically, given how much it could set back pro-Western reformers.[47] Only in a worst case, for example, one in which Iran developed nuclear weapons and also encouraged Hezbollah to dramatically escalate terrorist attacks against Israeli and Western interests, might the scenario be seriously contemplated.

But if some missions are simply not plausible, or barely so, a wide range is more thinkable than it might first appear. Given the nature of global terror, as well as the new dangers and continued spread of weapons of mass destruction, the United States may find itself in substantial and sustained military operations in places it would hardly have dreamed of only a short time ago. Several of the above scenarios would require significant numbers of ground forces, though not more than are in the American military today.

That said, and in conclusion, this book strongly advocates an expansion of the current capabilities of the U.S. Army and Marine Corps to deal with the ongoing and open-ended demands of the missions in Iraq and Afghanistan. The strategist is always tempted to think long term, and doing so is necessary. But today's armed forces have a compelling near-term challenge, to succeed in helping to stabilize Iraq and Afghanistan as well as possible without wearing out or breaking the all-volunteer military in the process. That objective must be at the heart of any defense planning exercise, inside or outside the government, carried out at this moment in history. It is the chief challenge of the U.S. armed forces today.

Notes

Chapter 1

1. Secretary Rumsfeld's Defense Science Board reached a similar conclusion. See Mark Mazzetti, "U.S. Military Is Stretched Too Thin, Defense Board Warns," *Los Angeles Times*, September 30, 2004.

2. Eric Schmitt, "General Says the Current Plan Is to Maintain 120,000 Soldiers in Iraq through 2006," *New York Times*, January 25, 2005.

3. See Jared Diamond, *Guns, Germs, and Steel* (New York: W. W. Norton, 1997).

4. Barry Posen, "Command of the Commons: The Military Foundation of U.S. Hegemony," *International Security* 28 (Summer 2003): 5–46; for a related argument, see Michael O'Hanlon, *Technological Change and the Future of Warfare* (Brookings, 2000), pp. 106–67.

5. On the importance of America's transparent system, see G. John Ikenberry, "Institutions, Strategic Restraint, and the Persistence of American Postwar Order," *International Security* 23 (Winter 1998–99): 43–78.

6. Matt Moore, "Worldwide Military Spending Up Sharply," *Philadelphia Inquirer*, June 10, 2004.

7. Department of Defense News Release, "National Guard and Reserve Mobilized as of February 25, 2004," February 25, 2004, available at www.defenselink.mil/releases/2004/nr20040225-0366.html. At that time, mobilized Army reservists totaled approximately 155,000; Air Force, 18,400; Marine Corps, 5,400; Navy, 2,300; and Coast Guard, 1,600.

8. John Diamond, "CIA's Spy Network Thin," *USA Today*, September 22, 2004, p. 13A.

9. See Posture Statement of General Richard B. Myers, Chairman of the Joint Chiefs of Staff, before the Senate Armed Services Committee, 108th Congress,

February 3, 2004; and Secretary of Defense Donald H. Rumsfeld, *Quadrennial Defense Review Report* (Department of Defense, September 30, 2001).

10. General Richard Myers, *National Military Strategy of the United States 2004* (Department of Defense, 2004), p. 18.

11. See Ivo H. Daalder and James M. Lindsay, *America Unbound: The Bush Revolution in Foreign Policy* (Brookings, 2003).

12. President George W. Bush, *The National Security Strategy of the United States* (White House, September 2002), pp. 13–17; for a critique, see Michael O'Hanlon, Susan Rice, and James Steinberg, *The New National Security Strategy and Preemption*, Policy Brief No. 113 (Brookings, January 2003).

13. For the original coinage of the term, see Richard N. Haass, "Wars of Choice," *Washington Post*, November 23, 2003.

14. See Michael O'Hanlon and Mike Mochizuki, *Crisis on the Korean Peninsula: How to Deal with a Nuclear North Korea* (New York: McGraw-Hill, 2003), pp. 1–55.

15. On arms control options, see Michael Levi and Michael O'Hanlon, *The Future of Arms Control* (Brookings, 2005). On missile defenses and next-generation sensor technology, see Michael E. O'Hanlon, *Technological Change and the Future of Warfare* (Brookings, 2000).

16. Myers, Posture Statement, p. 24.

17. Adam J. Hebert, "A Plague of Accidents," *Air Force Magazine*, February 2004, p. 59.

18. Prepared Statement of General John P. Jumper, Chief of Staff, U.S. Air Force, before the Senate Committee on Armed Services, February 10, 2004, p. 40.

19. Information provided to Brookings by George Reynolds, Marine Aviation Logistics Support Branch, through Marine Corps Lieutenant Colonel Sam Mundy, March 14, 2004.

20. Richard K. Betts, *Military Readiness: Concepts, Choices, Consequences* (Brookings, 1995), pp. 87–114; and Jason Forrester, Michael O'Hanlon, and Micah Zenko, "Measuring U.S. Military Readiness," *National Security Studies Quarterly* 7 (Spring 2001): 100–01.

21. Testimony of General John P. Abizaid, Commander, United States Central Command, before the Senate Committee on Armed Services, March 4, 2004, pp. 1, 7–8, available at www.senate.gov/~armed_services/testimony.cfm?wit_id=2312&id=1043.

22. As General Richard Myers put it, "During the FY 2004 budget cycle, Congress voiced concern over the Department's overseas basing plans. Since then, our global posture strategy has matured. We are now in the process of detailed consultation with our allies and members of Congress." See Myers, Posture Statement, p. 33.

23. Jonathan Weisman and Thomas E. Ricks, "Increase in War Funding Sought," *Washington Post*, October 26, 2004, p. 1; Steven M. Kosiak, "Final Action on the FY 2005 Defense Appropriations Act," *CSBA Update* (Washington: Center for Strategic and Budgetary Assessments, August 4, 2004), p. 1; and Steven M. Kosiak, "Funding for Defense, Military Operations, Homeland Security, and

Related Activities since 9/11," *CSBA Update* (Washington: Center for Strategic and Budgetary Assessments, October 18, 2004), p. 5.

24. Michael E. O'Hanlon, *Expanding Global Military Capacity for Humanitarian Intervention* (Brookings, 2003), pp. 56–57.

25. The total "050" or national security budget (essentially the DoD budget plus the cost of nuclear weapons activities of the Department of Energy) was $456 billion for 2003 and $461 billion for 2004, but those figures include supplemental appropriations for military operations of approximately $73 billion and $65 billion for the wars in Iraq and Afghanistan respectively and for certain homeland security emergency efforts. See House Committee on the Budget, "Fiscal Year 2004 Defense and Iraq and Afghanistan Reconstruction Emergency Supplemental Appropriations," November 5, 2003, available at www.budget. house.gov; House Resolution 1559, "Making Emergency Wartime Supplemental Appropriations for the Fiscal Year 2003," January 7, 2003, available at thomas.loc.gov/cgi-bin/query/C?c108:.temp; Jonathan Weisman, "Military Operations in Iraq Cost Nearly $4 Billion a Month," *Washington Post,* July 10, 2003, p. A24; and David Firestone, "The Struggle for Iraq: Senate Sends Spending Bill for War Costs to President," *New York Times,* November 4, 2003, p. A11.

26. R. L. Brownlee and General Peter J. Schoomaker, *Posture of the United States Army 2004* (Department of Defense, February 5, 2004), pp. 8–10.

27. Steven M. Kosiak, "Funding for Defense, Military Operations, Homeland Security, and Related Activities since 9/11," *CSBA Backgrounder* (Washington: Center for Strategic and Budgetary Assessments, January 21, 2004).

28. The estimate comes from former CIA official John MacGaffin; see James Risen, "How to Improve Domestic Intelligence," *New York Times,* April 18, 2004, p. WK5.

29. Testimony of General Bryan D. Brown, Commander, U.S. Special Operations Command, before the Subcommittee on Terrorism, Unconventional Threats, and Capabilities of the Committee on Armed Services of the U.S. House of Representatives, March 11, 2004, p. 8, available at www.house.gov/hasc; International Institute for Strategic Studies, *The Military Balance 2003/2004* (Oxford University Press, 2003), pp. 24–25; International Institute for Strategic Studies, *The Military Balance 2000/2001* (Oxford University Press, 2000), p. 31; and Department of Defense, "Special Operations Forces Posture Statement 2000," available at www.defenselink.mil/pubs/sof [January 3, 2005]).

30. Adam Talaber, *The Long-Term Implications of Current Defense Plans: Summary Update for Fiscal Year 2004* (Congressional Budget Office, July 2003), p. 2.

31. Peter A. Diamond and Peter R. Orszag, *Saving Social Security: A Balanced Approach* (Brookings, 2004), pp. 27–38.

32. Alice M. Rivlin and Isabel Sawhill, eds., *Restoring Fiscal Sanity: How to Balance the Budget* (Brookings, 2004), pp. 5–7.

33. Allison Percy, *Growth in Medical Spending by the Department of Defense* (Congressional Budget Office, 2003), pp. 1–2.

34. See Amy Belasco, *Paying for Military Readiness and Upkeep: Trends in Operation and Maintenance Spending* (Congressional Budget Office, 1997), p. 5;

and Lane Pierrot, *Budgeting for Defense: Maintaining Today's Forces* (Congressional Budget Office, 2000), pp. 18–23.

35. Tom Lantos, "Military Hardship Duty: Fill the 'Pay Gap' for National Guard and Reserves," *San Francisco Chronicle*, June 10, 2003, p. 23.

36. Steven M. Kosiak, *Analysis of the FY 2005 Defense Budget Request* (Washington: Center for Strategic and Budgetary Assessments, 2004), pp. 15–23.

37. Gregory T. Kiley, *The Effects of Aging on the Costs of Operating and Maintaining Military Equipment* (Congressional Budget Office, 2001); *Paying for Military Readiness and Upkeep: Trends in Operation and Maintenance Spending* (Congressional Budget Office, 1997).

38. Some optimists tend to exaggerate the savings from possible base closings, however. Wayne Glass, *Closing Military Bases: An Interim Assessment* (Congressional Budget Office, 1996).

39. Frances Lussier, *Options for Changing the Army's Overseas Basing* (Congressional Budget Office, 2004), p. xiv.

40. See Ellen Breslin-Davidson, *Restructuring Military Medical Care* (Congressional Budget Office, 1995); Russell Beland, *Accrual Budgeting for Military Retirees' Health Care* (Congressional Budget Office, 2002).

41. Robert F. Hale, *Promoting Efficiency in the Department of Defense: Keep Trying, but Be Realistic* (Washington: Center for Strategic and Budgetary Assessments, 2002).

42. P. W. Singer, *Corporate Warriors: The Rise of the Privatized Military Industry* (Cornell University Press, 2003).

43. Dave Ahearn, "12 Carriers Needed Despite Efficiencies—Admiral," *Defense Today*, July 9, 2004, p. 1.

44. For more on the debate about Europe versus America, see Robert Kagan, "Power and Weakness," *Policy Review* (June 2002); and Philip H. Gordon and Jeremy Shapiro, *Allies at War* (New York: McGraw-Hill, 2004).

45. For backup on those estimates, see John E. Peters and Howard Deshong, *Out of Area or Out of Reach? European Military Support for Operations in Southwest Asia* (Santa Monica, Calif.: RAND, 1995); Michael O'Hanlon, "Transforming NATO: The Role of European Forces," *Survival* 39 (Autumn 1997): 5–15; Congressional Budget Office, *NATO Burdensharing after Enlargement* (Washington, 2001).

Chapter 2

1. See Williamson Murray and Major General Robert H. Scales Jr., *The Iraq War: A Military History* (Harvard University Press, 2003).

2. Much of this is drawn from Michael O'Hanlon, "A Flawed Masterpiece: Assessing the Afghan Campaign," *Foreign Affairs* 81 (May-June 2002): 47–63.

3. For an excellent account of how the war strategy was devised, see Bob Woodward, *Bush at War* (New York: Simon and Schuster, 2002).

4. See Stephen Biddle, *Afghanistan and the Future of Warfare* (Carlisle, Pa.: Strategic Studies Institute, 2002), pp. 1–49.

5. See ABC News, "Prime Time: November 29, 2001," available at www.abcnews.com.

6. Biddle, *Afghanistan and the Future of Warfare*, pp. 43–58.

7. Andrew F. Krepinevich, *Operation Iraqi Freedom: A First-Blush Assessment* (Washington: Center for Strategic and Budgetary Assessments, 2003), pp. 18–19.

8. Richard J. Dunn III, Price T. Bingham, and Charles A. "Bert" Fowler, *Ground Moving Target Indicator Radar* (Rosslyn, Va.: Northrop Grumman, 2004), pp. 16–17.

9. David A. Fulghum and Robert Wall, "Baghdad Confidential," *Aviation Week and Space Technology* (April 28, 2003), p. 32.

10. On FBCB2 (essentially a combination of a GPS system, a specialized radio, and a computer), which was installed on all 4th Infantry Division vehicles and 100 to 200 vehicles of each of the other Army and Marine divisions; see Bruce T. Robinson, "Who Goes There?" *IEEE Spectrum* (October 2003), pp. 42–47.

11. Anthony H. Cordesman, *The Iraq War: Strategy, Tactics, and Military Lessons* (Washington: Center for Strategic and International Studies, 2003), pp. 365–67; Eric Schmitt, "In Iraq's Murky Battle, Snipers Offer U.S. a Precision Weapon," *New York Times*, January 2, 2004, p. 1.

12. See John Keegan, *The Iraq War* (New York: Alfred A. Knopf, 2004), pp. 165–219.

13. General Accounting Office, *Defense Logistics: Preliminary Observations on the Effectiveness of Logistics Activities during Operation Iraqi Freedom*, GAO-04-305R (December 2003), pp. 1–5.

14. See J. R. Wilson, "Logistics Fixes That Took Root," *Armed Forces Journal* (October 2003), pp. 44–50.

15. For the Army history, see Gregory Fontenot, E. J. Degen, and David Tohn, *On Point: The United States Army in Operation Iraqi Freedom* (Fort Leavenworth, Kans.: Combat Studies Institute Press, 2004), pp. 42–84.

16. Based on a quote from then-Secretary of the Army Thomas White in Michael R. Gordon, "The Strategy to Secure Iraq Did Not Foresee a 2nd War," *New York Times*, October 19, 2004, p. 1.

17. Frederick W. Kagan, "War and Aftermath," *Policy Review* (August–September 2003), pp. 3–27.

Chapter 3

1. Robert Wall, "Demand Pressure," *Aviation Week and Space Technology* (August 2, 2004), p. 31.

2. Adam J. Hebert, "Longer Deployments," *Air Force Magazine* (August 2004), p. 60.

3. Prepared Statement of General John P. Jumper, Chief of Staff, U.S. Air Force, before the Senate Committee on Armed Services, February 10, 2004, p. 8.

4. Testimony of Admiral Vernon E. Clark before the Senate Committee on Armed Services, February 10, 2004, pp. 6–13.

5. Esther Schrader, "Pentagon Scales Back Training Exercises Abroad," *Los Angeles Times*, August 16, 2003.

6. Posture Statement of General Richard B. Myers, Chairman of the Joint Chiefs of Staff, before the Senate Armed Services Committee, 108th Congress, February 3, 2004, p. 24.

7. Rowan Scarborough, "Army, in Tough Slog, Hits Recruiting Goal," *Washington Times*, September 30, 2004, p. 1; Associated Press, "Air Force Reserve Short in Recruiting," March 9, 2004 (www.washingtonpost.com); and Thomas E. Ricks, "Army Spouses Expect Reenlistment Problems," *Washington Post*, March 28, 2004, p. 1.

8. Eric Schmitt, "Its Recruitment Goals Pressing, the Army Will Ease Some Standards," *New York Times*, October 1, 2004; and Christopher Cooper and Greg Jaffe, "Army's Recruiters Miss Target for Enlistees in Latest Month," *Wall Street Journal*, October 20, 2004, p. 7.

9. Bruce D. Callander, "Force Shaping," *Air Force Magazine*, July 2004, pp. 58–62.

10. Lawrence J. Korb, "Fixing the Mix: How to Update the Army's Reserves," *Foreign Affairs* 83 (March-April 2004): 6.

11. Thomas E. Ricks, "In Army Survey, Troops in Iraq Report Low Morale," *Washington Post*, March 26, 2004, p. 18; and Ricks, "Army Spouses Expect Reenlistment Problems."

12. Dave Moniz, "Strained Army National Guard Having Tough Time Recruiting," *USA Today*, July 20, 2004, p. 5; and Richard Whittle, "As Army Holds Troops, Guard Loses Out," *Dallas Morning News*, October 20, 2004.

13. Thomas E. Ricks and Josh White, "Fewer Army Recruits Lined Up," *Washington Post*, July 22, 2004, p. A2.

14. Esther Schrader, "Pentagon Outlines Troop Rotation Plan for Iraq," *Los Angeles Times*, July 8, 2004.

15. Pat Towell, *Forging the Sword: Unit-Manning in the U.S. Army* (Washington: Center for Strategic and Budgetary Assessments, 2004), pp. 5, 11.

16. Brigadier General Larson, U.S. Army, Briefing at the Pentagon, February 11, 2004.

17. Under Secretary of Defense David Chu, "How Might We Think about Stress on the Force?" Briefing at the Pentagon, February 11, 2004.

18. See Michael O'Hanlon, *Defense Policy Choices for the Bush Administration* (Brookings, 2002), pp. 28–62.

19. See Remarks by President Bush to the United Nations, November 10, 2001, available at www.whitehouse.gov/news/releases/2001/11/print/20011110-3.html.

20. Under Secretary of Defense David Chu, "How Might We Think about Stress on the Force?"

21. Frances M. Lussier, *Structuring the Active and Reserve Army for the 21st Century* (Congressional Budget Office, 1997), p. 11.

22. See Eric Schmitt, "General Warns of a Looming Shortage of Specialists," *New York Times*, September 17, 2004.

23. Barton Gellman and Dafna Linzer, "Afghanistan, Iraq: Two Wars Collide," *Washington Post*, October 22, 2004, p. A1.

24. Susan L. Marquis, *Unconventional Warfare: Rebuilding U.S. Special Operations Forces* (Brookings, 1997), pp. 4–5.

25. Michael Fitzsimmons, "The Importance of Being Special: Planning for the Future of U.S. Special Operations Forces," *Defense and Security Analysis* 19 (September 2003): 203–18.

26. Marquis, *Unconventional Warfare*, pp. 4–5, 261–70.

27. Brigadier General Larson, U.S. Army, Briefing at the Pentagon, February 11, 2004.

28. Douglas A. Macgregor, "XVIII Airborne Corps: Spearhead of Military Transformation," *Defense Horizons* (January 2004).

29. Richard Whittle, "General: Iraq 'Stretching the Army,'" *Dallas Morning News*, July 13, 2004.

30. See Donald H. Rumsfeld, "Rumors about a Draft Are False," *Salt Lake City Desert News*, October 28, 2004.

31. Thom Shanker and Eric Schmitt, "Army May Reduce Length of Tours in Combat Zones," *New York Times*, September 27, 2004, p. 1.

32. Vernon Loeb, "Army Expansion Could Last 5 Years," *Washington Post*, January 30, 2004, p. 19.

33. "Army's Third Infantry Division Is Ordered to Return to Iraq," *Washington Post*, July 25, 2004, p. A9.

34. Tony Perry, "Back from a Hot Spot, Marines Feel the Warmth," *Los Angeles Times*, July 16, 2004.

35. James R. Helmly, "A Streamlined Army Reserve," *Washington Post*, September 22, 2003, p. 23.

36. James Kitfield, "In a Time of War," *Air Force Magazine* (July 2004), pp. 23–28; U.S. Department of Defense, "News Release: National Guard and Reserve Mobilized as of September 29, 2004," no. 966-04, September 29, 2004, available at www.defenselink.mil/releases/2004/nr20040929-1333.html; and Brigadier General Larson, U.S. Army, Briefing at the Pentagon, February 11, 2004; and Under Secretary of Defense David Chu, "How Might We Think about Stress on the Force?" Briefing at the Pentagon, February 11, 2004.

37. For historical evidence that such trends are largely what is to be expected in stabilization and nation building efforts, see James Dobbins and others, *America's Role in Nation-Building: From Germany to Iraq* (Santa Monica, Calif.: RAND, 2003), p. xvii. But it is important to underscore that no two drawdowns look the same and that the Iraq mission combines stabilization and nation building efforts with counterinsurgency in a way that most previous operations have not. With Iraq in particular, see also Tom Bowman, "Ceding Iraq, Keeping Troops," *Baltimore Sun*, February 20, 2004.

38. For generally persuasive recommendations along these lines, see Clark A. Murdock and others, *Beyond Goldwater-Nichols: Defense Reform for a New Strategic Era*, Phase 1 Report (Washington: Center for Strategic and International Studies, 2004).

39. See Fitzsimmons, "The Importance of Being Special."

40. For more on these and other similar ideas, see Cindy Williams, ed., *Filling the Ranks: Transforming the U.S. Military Personnel System* (MIT Press, 2004), especially pp. 303–31.

41. Adebayo Adedeji and others, *An Analysis of the U.S. Military's Ability to Sustain an Occupation of Iraq* (Congressional Budget Office, September 2003), pp. 3, 19.

42. On costs, note that an increase of 40,000 soldiers is about an 8 percent increase in the active force. The total Army budget is about $100 billion, of which some $85 billion is for the active force, so an 8 percent increase could be expected to translate into about $7 billion—though exact amounts would, of course, depend on what equipment was purchased and also how quickly it needed to be purchased. See Office of the Under Secretary of Defense (Comptroller), *National Defense Budget Estimates for FY 2005* (2004), pp. 103, 127.

Chapter 4

1. See for example, Max Boot, "Shouldering the Load, and the Rifle," *Los Angeles Times*, February 26, 2004; and U.S. Commission on National Security/21st Century, *Seeking a National Strategy: A Concert for Preserving Security and Promoting Freedom* (Washington: U.S. Commission on National Security/21st Century, 2002).

2. Richard K. Betts, "The Delusion of Impartial Intervention," *Foreign Affairs* 73 (November/December 1994): 20–33; and Stephen John Stedman, "Alchemy for a New World Order," *Foreign Affairs* 74 (May/June 1995): 17–18.

3. Peace through Law Education Fund, *A Force for Peace and Security: U.S. and Allied Commanders' Views of the Military's Role in Peace Operations and the Impact on Terrorism of States in Conflict* (Washington, 2002), p. 9.

4. Michael O'Hanlon, *Saving Lives with Force* (Brookings, 1997).

5. Robert M. Perito, *Where Is the Lone Ranger When We Need Him?* (Washington: U.S. Institute of Peace, 2004), pp. 323–37.

6. See for example, Jane Harman, "Four Steps to Better Intelligence," *Washington Post*, February 8, 2004, p. B7.

7. See James T. Quinlivan, "Force Requirements in Stability Operations," *Parameters* 25 (Winter 1995–1996): 59–69.

8. I am grateful to Lael Brainard and Susan Rice for help in thinking through this problem; see also Alice M. Rivlin and Isabel Sawhill, eds., *Restoring Fiscal Sanity: How to Balance the Budget* (Brookings, 2004), pp. 46–51; Testimony of Michael Sheehan before the Senate Foreign Relations Committee, April 21, 2004; and U.S. Institute of Peace, "Building Civilian Capacity for U.S. Stability Operations: The Rule of Law Component," *U.S. Institute of Peace Special Report No. 118* (Washington, April 2004).

9. See "Should the Draft Be Reinstated?" *Time*, December 29, 2003, p. 101.

10. Helen Dewar, "Hagel Seeking Broad Debate on Draft Issue," *Washington Post*, April 22, 2004, p. 25.

11. See Donald H. Rumsfeld, "Rumors about a Draft Are False," *Salt Lake City Desert News*, October 28, 2004.

12. Ole R. Holsti, "A Widening Gap between the U.S. Military and Civilian Society? Some Evidence, 1976–1996," *International Security* 23 (Winter 1998–99): 13.

13. David C. King and Zachary Karabell, *The Generation of Trust: How the U.S. Military Has Regained the Public's Confidence since Vietnam* (Washington: American Enterprise Institute, 2003), p. 44.

14. Center for Strategic and International Studies, *American Military Culture in the Twenty-First Century* (Washington, 2000), pp. 32–33.

15. Adebayo Adedeji, *Educational Attainment and Compensation of Enlisted Personnel* (Congressional Budget Office, 2004), p. 14.

16. King and Karabell, *The Generation of Trust*.

17. On the latter figure, see Dave Moniz and Tom Squitieri, "Front-Line Troops Disproportionately White, Not Black," *USA Today*, January 21, 2003, p. 1. Some additional statistics: enlisted personnel are 85 percent male and 15 percent female, and 50 percent of all enlistees are married. The enlisted force consists of 95 percent high school graduates and 5 percent GED holders. The officer corps is 8.3 percent African American and about 4 percent Hispanic, meaning that minority officer representation is far from proportional to the racial profile of the enlisted force but much greater than for many other professions in the United States. The officer corps is also highly educated, with 91 percent holding at least a bachelor's degree and 11 percent of the total holding a higher degree as well. See Department of Defense, *Population Representation in the Military Services* (2001), available at www.defenselink.mil/prhome/poprep2001/chapter3/chpater3_6.htm.

18. For a good overview of how one U.S. military service improved dramatically after Vietnam, see Robert H. Scales Jr., *Certain Victory: The U.S. Army in the Gulf War* (Washington: Brassey's, 1994), pp. 1–38.

19. For a description of the total force policy of the post-Vietnam era, see Michael D. Doubler, *I Am the Guard: A History of the Army National Guard, 1636–2000* (Government Printing Office, 2001), pp. 269–300; see also Janine Davidson, "A Citizen Check on War," *Washington Post*, November 16, 2003, p. B7.

20. For a review of the debate of that time, see Steven Kull and I. M. Destler, *Misreading the Public: The Myth of a New Isolationism* (Brookings, 1999), pp. 81–112.

21. For an illuminating study of why military service should be viewed as a profession, albeit one with its problems, see Don M. Snider and Gayle L. Watkins, project directors, and Lloyd J. Matthews, ed., *The Future of the Army Profession* (New York: McGraw-Hill, 2002).

22. Lane Pierrot, *Structuring U.S. Forces after the Cold War: Costs and Effects of Increased Reliance on the Reserves* (Congressional Budget Office, September 1992).

23. Associated Press, "National Guard in Short Supply, Some States Fear," *Honolulu Advertiser*, May 17, 2004.

24. Esther Schrader, "U.S. Seeks Military Access in N. Africa," *Los Angeles Times*, March 27, 2004.

25. For a similar argument, see Thomas Donnelly and Vance Serchuk, "Toward a Global Cavalry: Overseas Rebasing and Defense Transformation," *National Security Outlook* (July 2003).

26. See Testimony by Secretary of Defense Donald H. Rumsfeld before the Senate Committee on Armed Services, "Global Posture Review of the United States Military Forces Stationed Overseas," September 23, 2004, p. 7 (of 57).

27. Bradley Graham, "U.S. May Halve Forces in Germany," *Washington Post*, March 25, 2004, p. A1; and Michael R. Gordon, "A Pentagon Plan Would Cut Back G.I.s in Germany," *New York Times*, June 4, 2004, p. 1.

28. Andrew Koch, "U.S. Troops on the Move Towards Faster and More Flexible Deployment," *Jane's Defence Weekly*, August 25, 2004.

29. For more on this, see Richard Halloran, "U.S. Pacific Command Facing Sweeping Changes," *Washington Times*, February 2, 2004, p. 11.

30. See Michael O'Hanlon and Mike Mochizuki, *Crisis on the Korean Peninsula: How to Deal with a Nuclear North Korea* (New York: McGraw-Hill, 2003).

31. For more on this, see O'Hanlon and Mochizuki, *Crisis on the Korean Peninsula*.

32. Posture Statement of General Richard B. Myers, Chairman of the Joint Chiefs of Staff, before the Senate Armed Services Committee, 108th Congress, February 3, 2004, p. 33.

33. President Bush probably overstated the morale benefits in his August 2004 speech on the subject. See Mike Allen and Josh White, "President Outlines Overseas Troop Cut," *Washington Post*, August 17, 2004, p. 1.

34. Frances Lussier, *Options for Changing the Army's Overseas Basing* (Congressional Budget Office, 2004), p. xiv.

35. Michael R. Gordon, "U.S. Weighs Cutback in Forces in Germany," *International Herald Tribune*, June 4, 2004, p. 1.

36. For a good description of the recent troubles there, including the tortured effort to relocate the Futenma Marine Air Station, see Takehiko Kambayashi, "U.S. Base's Transfer on Hold," *Washington Times*, March 26, 2004, p. 18.

37. On the Australia notion, see Rod Lyon and William T. Tow, *The Future of the Australian-U.S. Security Relationship* (Carlisle, Pa.: Strategic Studies Institute, U.S. Army War College, 2003), p. 30.

38. Statement of General James L. Jones, USMC, Commander, U.S. European Command, before the Senate Armed Services Committee, March 4, 2004, p. 6.

39. Julian Lindley-French and Franco Algieri, *A European Defence Strategy* (Guetersloh, Germany: Bertelsmann Foundation, May 2004), p. 10.

40. Lakhdar Brahimi and others, "Report of the Panel on United Nations Peace Keeping Operations," A/55/305-2/200/809 (New York: United Nations, August 21, 2000).

41. Bradley Graham, "Bush Plans Aid to Build Foreign Peace Forces," *Washington Post*, April 19, 2004, p. A1.

42. See Michael E. O'Hanlon and Susan E. Rice, "Stopping the Next Genocide" (www.yaleglobal.edu [April 2, 2004]).

43. See "G-8 Action Plan: Expanding Global Capability for Peace Support Operations," Sea Island, Georgia, June 2004, available at www.g8usa.gov/d_061004c.htm.

44. On NATO's capability, see Raymond A. Millen, *Reconfiguring the American Military Presence in Europe* (Carlisle, Pa.: Strategic Studies Institute, Army War College, 2004), pp. 25–26.

Chapter 5

1. See, most notably, Admiral William A. Owens with Ed Offley, *Lifting the Fog of War* (New York: Farrar, Straus, and Giroux, 2000).

2. National Defense Panel, *Transforming Defense* (Washington, 1997), pp. 7–8.

3. See Michael O'Hanlon, *Technological Change and the Future of Warfare* (Brookings, 2000), pp. 32–105.

4. Ibid., p. 29.

5. Greg Jaffe, "Planning for Big Battles, Army Snubbed a Humvee Model Built for Guerilla Fights: 'We Didn't Anticipate' Threat," *Wall Street Journal*, March 29, 2004, p. 1; Vernon Loeb and Theola Labbe, "Body Armor Saves Lives in Iraq: Pentagon Criticized for Undersupply of Protective Vests," *Washington Post*, December 4, 2003, p. 1; and Philip Dine, "Guard Gets Shortchanged, Army Admits," *St. Louis Post-Dispatch*, December 28, 2003, p. 1.

6. Hal Bernton, "Lack of Vehicle Armor Keeps Troops on Edge," *Seattle Times*, October 21, 2004, p. 1.

7. Graham T. Allison, Paul X. Kelley, and Richard L. Garwin, *Nonlethal Weapons and Capabilities* (New York: Council on Foreign Relations, 2004), p. 2; and Amy Svitak, "Pentagon Transformation Leader Suggests Improvements," *National Journal's Congress Daily*, December 3, 2003.

8. Dave Ahearn, "Admiral Giambastiani Slams Defense Industry, Mid-Level Procurement Officers," *Defense Today*, August 5, 2004, p. 1.

9. James M. Lindsay and Michael E. O'Hanlon, *Defending America: The Case for Limited National Missile Defense* (Brookings, 2001), p. 6.

10. Associated Press, "Missile Interceptor Installed in Alaska," *Los Angeles Times*, July 23, 2004.

11. Tony Capaccio, "Lockheed Upgrading Destroyers to Monitor North Korea," July 15, 2004 (www.bloomberg.com [August 1, 2004]).

12. Jonathan S. Landay, "U.S. Ponders Antimissile Site in Eastern Europe," *Miami Herald*, June 28, 2004.

13. Gopal Ratnam, "No Missile Defense Shield in Space, For Now: Kadish," March 23, 2004 (www.defensenews.com [August 1, 2004]).

14. Missile Defense Agency, "Press Release: Fiscal Year 2005 Budget Estimates," February 18, 2004 (www.acq.osd.mil/bmdo/bmdolink/html/guide.html).

15. See Bradley Graham, "Interceptor System Set, but Doubts Remain," *Washington Post*, September 29, 2004, p. 1.

16. James Glanz, "Pointed Questions on Missile Defense System," *New York Times*, March 12, 2004.

17. See Geoffrey Forden, *Budgetary and Technical Implications of the Administration's Plan for National Missile Defense* (Congressional Budget Office, 2000), p. 10; Lindsay and O'Hanlon, *Defending America*, p. 115.

18. Jeremy Singer and Warren Ferster, "MDA Request Cancels Ramos, Slows Work on Space Interceptors," *Space News*, February 16, 2004, p. 7; and Randy Barrett, "Critics Say Sea-Based Missile Needs Complete Overhaul," *Space News*, October 27, 2003, p. 9.

19. Gopal Ratnam, "Technical and Budget Issues May Ground Airborne Laser," *Space News*, July 12, 2004, p. 6.

20. Michael O'Hanlon, *Neither Star Wars nor Sanctuary: Constraining the Military Uses of Space* (Brookings, 2004).

21. Bill Gertz, "Signal Jamming a Factor in Future Wars, General Says," *Washington Times*, July 16, 2004, p. 10.

22. See Loren Thompson, "Satellites over Iraq," *Intelligence, Surveillance, and Reconnaissance Journal* 3 (March 2004): 16–20. Gertz, "Signal Jamming a Factor in Future Wars," p. 10; and O'Hanlon, *Neither Star Wars nor Sanctuary*.

23. Jeremy Singer, "Panel Says Space Based Radar May Be Ineffective, Too Expensive," *Space News*, June 21, 2004, p. 1.

24. See Edmond Lococo, "U.S. Air Force Anti-Satellite Weapon Is Operational," September 30, 2004 (www.bloomberg.com [October 1, 2004]).

25. Steven M. Kosiak, *Matching Resources with Requirements: Options for Modernizing the U.S. Air Force* (Washington: Center for Strategic and Budgetary Assessments, 2004), p. 41.

26. For good information sources on these and other weapons programs, see the database maintained by John Pike of GlobalSecurity.org (www.globalsecurity.org/military/systems [January 4, 2005]).

27. Anthony H. Cordesman, *The Iraq War: Strategy, Tactics, and Military Lessons* (Washington: Center for Strategic and International Studies Press, 2003), p. 254.

28. David A. Fulghum and Robert Wall, "Prices at the Pump," *Aviation Week and Space Technology*, March 22, 2004, p. 27.

29. Bill Sweetman, "In the Tracks of the Predator: Combat UAV Programs Are Gathering Speed," *Jane's International Defence Review* (August 2004), pp. 48–55.

30. Donald C. Daniel, "The Air Force: Science, Technology, and Transformation," *Defense Horizons*, no. 27 (Washington: National Defense University, May 2003), p. 6.

31. Hampton Stephens, "USAF: Indian Exercises Showed Need for F/A-22, Changes in Training," *Inside the Air Force*, June 4, 2004, p. 1.

32. Robert Wall, "Changing Story," *Aviation Week and Space Technology*, May 10, 2004, p. 35.

33. Alderman and Company, *First Quarter Newsletter* (2004), New York (www.aldermanco.com).

34. Michael Sirak, "U.S. Air Force to Buy STOVL Variant of Fighter," *Jane's Defence Weekly*, February 18, 2004, p. 6.

35. Congressional Budget Office, *Budget Options* (March 2003), pp. 25–26.

36. For a fuller discussion, see Michael Levi and Michael O'Hanlon, *The Future of Arms Control* (Brookings, 2004).

37. Congressional Budget Office, *The Bomb's Custodians* (1994); and Congressional Budget Office, *Budget Options* (March 2003), pp. 31–32.

38. Walter Pincus, "Defense Panel Faults Nuclear Plans," *Washington Post*, March 28, 2004, p. 4; and Michael A. Levi, "Learning to Love the Tiny Bomb?" *Foreign Policy*, March-April 2004.

39. For more, see Christopher Paine, "It Really Is the Pits," *Bulletin of the Atomic Scientists* (September-October 2003), p. 73.

40. General Barry R. McCaffrey, "Joint Firepower Wins Wars," *Armed Forces Journal* (October 2003): 8–10.

41. See, for example, Department of the Army, *Army Modernization Plan 2003*, pp. 47–52, D-24 through D-25.

42. Renae Merle, "Army Raises Cost of Combat Modernization," *Washington Post*, July 23, 2004, p. 23.

43. Statement of Paul L. Francis, Director, Acquisition and Sourcing Management, General Accounting Office, *Defense Acquisitions: The Army's Future Combat Systems' Features, Risks, and Alternatives*, GAO-04-635T (April 1, 2004), pp. 1–7.

44. Joshua Kucera, "Iraq Conflict Raises Doubts on FCS Survivability," *Jane's Defence Weekly*, May 19, 2004, p. 8.

45. For concurring views, see F. Stephen Larrabee, John Gordon IV, and Peter A. Wilson, "The Right Stuff," *National Interest* 77 (Fall 2004), p. 58; and Joseph N. Mait and Richard L. Kugler, "Alternative Approaches to Army Transformation," *Defense Horizons*, no. 41 (Washington: National Defense University, 2004), p. 1.

46. See Peter A. Wilson, John Gordon IV, and David E. Johnson, "An Alternative Future Force: Building a Better Army," *Parameters* (Winter 2003–04): 19–39. The question of the Stryker's weight—one example of the type of issue that needs to be studied—remains open. It may be too heavy for easy air transport in C-130 aircraft. See Thomas E. Ricks, "GAO Calls Stryker Too Heavy for Transport," *Washington Post*, August 14, 2004, p. 4.

47. Department of Defense, *Program Acquisition Costs by Weapon System* (February 2004), p. 49; and Congressional Budget Office, *Budget Options* (March 2003), p. 14.

48. Lieutenant Colonel Kevin Gross, "Dispelling the Myth of the V-22," *Proceedings* (September 2004), pp. 38–41.

49. Elaine M. Grossman, "Christie: V-22's 'Vortex Ring State' May Yet Pose Operational Problems," *Inside the Pentagon*, December 18, 2003, p. 3.

50. Comments of Assistant Secretary of Defense David S. C. Chu at a special hearing before a subcommittee of the Committee on Appropriations of the United States Senate, July 19, 1990, Senate Hearing 101-934, 101 Cong., 2 sess., p. 51; and L. Dean Simmons, "Assessment of Alternatives for the V-22 Assault Aircraft

Program," Institute for Defense Analyses, June 1990, Senate Hearing 101-934, p. 17.

51. See Michael O'Hanlon, *Defense Policy Choices for the Bush Administration*, 2nd ed. (Brookings, 2002), pp. 117–119.

52. Allison, Kelley, and Garwin, *Nonlethal Weapons and Capabilities*, pp. 1–2.

53. Robert Wall, "Weighty Decisions," *Aviation Week and Space Technology*, March 22, 2004, p. 26; and David A. Fulghum and Robert Wall, "Escalation," *Aviation Week and Space Technology*, March 22, 2004, pp. 24–25.

54. On this idea, see Senior Chief David L. Davenport, U.S. Navy, "Abolish Sea-Shore Rotation," *Proceedings* (April 2004), pp. 46–48; and William F. Morgan, *Rotate Crews, Not Ships* (Alexandria, Va.: Center for Naval Analyses, June 1994), pp. 1–9.

55. Guy Gugliotta, "Radical Warship Takes Shape," *Washington Post*, February 8, 2004, p. 3.

56. Congressional Budget Office, *Budget Options* (March 2003), pp. 19–20.

57. Andrew Koch, "U.S. Navy Tackles Submarine Dilemma," *Jane's Defence Weekly*, June 23, 2004, p. 7.

58. Congressional Budget Office, *Budget Options* (March 2003), pp. 17–18.

59. Andrew Koch, "Personnel Cuts Head USN Strategy to Boost Fleet," *Jane's Defence Weekly*, January 21, 2004, p. 8.

60. I am grateful to Lane Pierrot for coining the term *silver bullet* in this context.

Chapter 6

1. See William W. Kaufmann, *Assessing the Base Force: How Much Is Too Much?* (Brookings, 1992), pp. 17–72.

2. See Michael O'Hanlon, *Defense Planning for the Late 1990s: Beyond the Desert Storm Framework* (Brookings, 1995), pp. 42–78; and Michael O'Hanlon, *How to Be a Cheap Hawk: The 1999 and 2000 Defense Budgets* (Brookings, 1998), pp. 52–76.

3. Secretary of Defense Donald Rumsfeld, *Quadrennial Defense Review Report* (Department of Defense, 2001), p. 21.

4. Ibid., pp. 17–22.

5. For a somewhat similar list, see Paul K. Davis, *Analytic Architecture for Capabilities-Based Planning, Mission-System Analysis, and Transformation* (Santa Monica, Calif.: RAND Corporation, 2002), p. 16.

6. Reportedly, Pentagon models estimate about 50,000 U.S. and 500,000 South Korean military casualties during the first three months of war. See Don Oberdorfer, "A Minute to Midnight," *Newsweek*, October 20, 1997, p. 18.

7. Secretary of Defense Les Aspin, *Report on the Bottom-Up Review* (Department of Defense, October 1993), pp. 13–22; and Secretary of Defense William S. Cohen, *Report of the Quadrennial Defense Review,* Department of Defense, May 1997), pp. 12–13, 24–26, 30.

8. On North Korea's defense budget, see Bill Gertz, "North Korea Pumps Money into Military," *Washington Times*, August 3, 2004, p. 1.

9. On the comparison with Europe, see, for example, Fran Lussier, *U.S. Ground Forces and the Conventional Balance in Europe* (Congressional Budget Office, June 1988), pp. 7–28, 91–99. About one-fourth of the total NATO and Warsaw Pact forces were either deployed in the Germany-Poland-Czechoslovakia area or immediately deployable to that zone using prepositioned stocks. That made for a total of roughly 2.5 million troops and 60,000 armored vehicles in a zone with a front three times the length of the Korean DMZ—similar numbers, per kilometer of front, to what prevails near the DMZ. But forces in East and West Germany, Poland, and Czechoslovakia were based as far away as 200 to 300 kilometers from the East-West German border, whereas most of those in North and South Korea are within roughly 100 kilometers of the front. See also, James C. Wendt, "U.S. Conventional Arms Control for Korea: A Proposed Approach," RAND Note (Santa Monica, Calif.: RAND Corporation, 1993), p. 14; Don Oberdorfer, *The Two Koreas*, new ed. (New York, Basic Books, 2001), p. 313; and U.S. Defense Intelligence Agency, *North Korea: The Foundations for Military Strength: Update 1995* (March 1996), p. 13.

10. Nick Beldecos and Eric Heginbotham, "The Conventional Military Balance in Korea," *Breakthroughs* (Spring 1995), p. 3; and Yong-Sup Han, "Designing and Evaluating Conventional Arms Control Measures: The Case of the Korean Peninsula" (Santa Monica, Calif.: RAND Corporation, 1993), pp. 31, 155.

11. Ministry of National Defense, Republic of Korea, *Defense White Paper 2000* (Seoul, 2000), pp. 47–49; and Kongdan Oh and Ralph C. Hassig, *North Korea through the Looking Glass* (Brookings, 2000), pp. 110–111.

12. North Korea has about 500 artillery tubes within range of Seoul. Each could fire one or more rounds a minute at the South Korean capital over an extended period. Unless virtually all their locations were known in advance, permitting preemptive attack, U.S. and ROK forces would be able to destroy them only after observing the trajectories of the shells they launched and then firing weapons at those locations. Even in a best case for coalition forces, a typical North Korean weapon would be able to fire several shots before being destroyed.

13. See "Lessons from the Iraq War: Strategy and Planning," *Strategic Comments* 9 (May 2003).

14. Such ideas have reportedly been investigated in regard to Korea (and Pyongyang surely has figured that out); see Thom Shanker, "Lessons from Iraq Include How to Scare North Korean Leader," *New York Times*, May 12, 2003.

15. See Bill Gertz, "Admiral Says Taiwan Invasion Would Fail," *Washington Times*, March 8, 2000, p. A5; Harold Brown, Joseph W. Prueher, and Adam Segal, eds., *Chinese Military Power* (New York: Council on Foreign Relations, 2003), pp. 27–28; Tony Capaccio, "China Has Boosted Military, U.S. General Says," January 13, 2004 (www.bloomberg.com); David Shambaugh, *Modernizing China's Military* (University of California Press, 2002), pp. 328–30; and Michael O'Hanlon, *Defense Policy Choices for the Bush Administration*, 2nd ed. (Brookings, 2002), pp. 154-203. The Pentagon is somewhat more worried about the invasion option but does not disagree with the assertion that it would be very challenging,

largely because of lift constraints, and probably not China's preferred option. See Department of Defense, "FY04 Report to Congress Pursuant to the FY2000 National Defense Authorization Act: Annual Report on the Military Power of the People's Republic of China," 2004, pp. 46–52. See also Michael D. Swaine and Ashley J. Tellis, *Interpreting China's Grand Strategy* (Santa Monica, Calif.: RAND, 2000), p. 167.

16. Lyle Goldstein and William Murray, "Undersea Dragons: China's Maturing Submarine Force," *International Security* 28 (Spring 2004): 161–96; and Michael A. Glosny, "Strangulation from the Sea: A PRC Submarine Blockade of Taiwan," *International Security* 28 (Spring 2004): 125–60.

17. The number was estimated at 500 as of 2003. See Department of Defense, "FY04 Report to Congress on the Military Power of the People's Republic of China," p. 6.

18. Michael A. Glosny, "Mines against Taiwan: A Military Analysis of a PRC Blockade," *Breakthroughs* (Spring 2003): 31–40.

19. For a somewhat similar assessment, see Richard A. Bitzinger and Bates Gill, *Gearing Up for High-Tech Warfare? Chinese and Taiwanese Defense Modernization and Implications for Military Confrontation across the Taiwan Strait, 1995–2005* (Washington: Center for Strategic and Budgetary Assessments, 1996), pp. 44–5.

20. Ian Storey and You Ji, "China's Aircraft Carrier Ambitions," *Naval War College Review* (Winter 2004), pp. 77–94.

21. See E. R. Hooton, ed., *Jane's Naval Weapon Systems*, no. 30 (Alexandria, Va.: Jane's Information Group, August 1999).

22. Ronald Montaperto, "China," in *1997 Strategic Assessment*, edited by Patrick Clawson (Washington: National Defense University, 1996), p. 52; and William S. Cohen, "The Security Situation in the Taiwan Strait: Report to Congress Pursuant to the FY99 Appropriations Bill" (Department of Defense, 1999), pp. 9, 16–17.

23. Captain Richard Sharpe, ed., *Jane's Fighting Ships 1995–96* (Alexandria, Va.: Jane's Information Group, 1995), pp. 117–118.

24. Anthony J. Watts, *Jane's Underwater Warfare Systems, 1998–99*, 10th ed. (Alexandria, Va.: Jane's Information Group, 1998), pp. 215–16.

25. Karl Lautenschlager, "The Submarine in Naval Warfare, 1901–2001," *International Security* 11 (Winter 1986–87): 258–68.

26. Eric McVadon, "PRC Exercises, Doctrine, and Tactics toward Taiwan: The Naval Dimension," in *Crisis in the Taiwan Strait*, edited by James R. Lilley and Chuck Downs (Washington: National Defense University Press, 1997), pp. 259–62.

27. See for example, Andrew F. Krepinevich Jr., *The Conflict Environment of 2016: A Scenario-Based Approach* (Washington: Center for Strategic and Budgetary Assessments, 1996), p. 7.

28. Peter Yu Kien-hong, "Taking Taiwan," *Jane's Intelligence Review* (September 1998): 31–32; Sharpe, ed., *Jane's Fighting Ships 1995–96*, pp. 116–118, 700–701; and Glosny, "Strangulation from the Sea?" pp. 139–47.

29. O'Hanlon, *Defense Policy Choices*, pp. 154–203.

30. Goldstein and Murray, "Undersea Dragons," pp. 161–96.

31. Hans Binnendijk and Stuart E. Johnson, *Transforming for Stabilization and Reconstruction Operations* (Washington: National Defense University, 2004), p. 41.

32. See Martin Indyk, "A Trusteeship for Palestine?" *Foreign Affairs* 82 (May–June 2003), pp. 51–66.

33. International Institute for Strategic Studies, *The Military Balance 2003–2004* (Oxford University Press, 2003), pp. 278, 336, 346–47.

34. See Sumit Ganguly, *Conflict Unending: India-Pakistan Tensions since 1947* (Columbia University Press, 2001).

35. See Stephen Philip Cohen, *The Idea of Pakistan* (Brookings, 2004), pp. 97–130.

36. See International Crisis Group, *Unfulfilled Promises: Pakistan's Failure to Tackle Extremism* (Brussels, 2004).

37. International Institute for Strategic Studies, *The Military Balance 2003–2004*, pp. 140–42.

38. Ibid., pp. 136–37, 337.

39. On Indonesia, see Robert Karniol, "Country Briefing: Indonesia," *Jane's Defence Weekly*, April 7, 2004, pp. 47–52.

40. Krepinevich, *The Conflict Environment of 2016*, pp. 23-27.

41. Energy Information Administration factsheets, Department of Energy, 2002 (www.eia.doe.gov/emeu/cabs/topworldtables1_2.html).

42. Thomas L. McNaugher, *Arms and Oil: U.S. Military Strategy and the Persian Gulf* (Brookings, 1985), pp. 1–18; 160–206.

43. Joshua M. Epstein, *Conventional Force Reductions: A Dynamic Assessment* (Brookings, 1990), pp. 51–65.

44. Gregory Fontenot, E. J. Degen, and David Tohn, *On Point: The United States Army in Operation Iraqi Freedom* (Fort Leavenworth, Kans.: Combat Studies Institute Press), pp. 209–21.

45. Krepinevich, *The Conflict Environment of 2016*, pp. 11–15.

46. International Institute for Strategic Studies, *The Military Balance 2003–2004*, p. 110.

47. On past government consideration of this option, see Richard A. Clarke, *Against All Enemies: Inside America's War on Terror* (New York: Free Press, 2004), p. 284.

Index

ACRI. *See* African Crisis Response Initiative

Afghanistan: border with Pakistan, 32–33; rebuilding, 42; stabilization force, 29, 42, 65; Taliban rule, 111. *See also* Operation Enduring Freedom

Afghanistan, U.S. forces in: need for continued presence, 2, 40, 120; number of, 11, 28; Operation Anaconda, 28, 29; supplemental appropriations for, 13

Africa: al Qaeda presence, 60, 71; improving crisis response capability, 68–70; Operation Focus Relief, 70; potential stabilization missions, 113–14; Rwanda genocide, 69, 70; training for militaries, 24, 69–70; U.S. troop presence, 60

African Americans, in military, 56

African Crisis Response Initiative (ACRI), 69

African Union, 70, 71

Aircraft: airlift, 84; B-1 bombers, 35, 87; C-130s, 89; C-17s, 37; F-15s, 85, 86; F-16s, 85, 87; F/A-22 Raptors, 85–86; fighters, 84–86; joint strike fighter, 85, 87, 91; JSTARS (joint surveillance and target attack radar system), 30, 35, 82; stealthy, 9, 85–86; tankers, 84; unmanned aerial vehicles, 9, 30, 33, 85, 87; V-22 tilt-rotor, 90–91

Aircraft carriers, 24, 30, 40

Air Expeditionary Forces, 39–40

Air Force: Air Expeditionary Forces, 39–40; B-1 bombers, 35, 87; enforcement of Iraqi no-fly zones, 39; involvement in Iraq war, 39; Okinawa base, 108; readiness, 10; recruiting targets, 41; reducing number of personnel, 41; retention, 41; weapons modernization programs, 84–88

Air Force National Guard, 57–59

Allies: burden sharing, 23–25, 64–66; coalition forces in Iraq, 25, 64, 71; collective security, 16; European, 2, 24; lack of consultation by Bush administration, 62; power projec-

ℬ THE BROOKINGS INSTITUTION

The Brookings Institution is an independent organization devoted to nonpartisan research, education, and publication in economics, government, foreign policy, and the social sciences generally. Its principal purposes are to aid in the development of sound public policies and to promote public understanding of issues of national importance. The Institution was founded on December 8, 1927, to merge the activities of the Institute for Government Research, founded in 1916, the Institute of Economics, founded in 1922, and the Robert Brookings Graduate School of Economics and Government, founded in 1924. The Institution maintains a position of neutrality on issues of public policy to safeguard the intellectual freedom of the staff. Interpretations or conclusions in Brookings publications should be understood to be solely those of the authors.